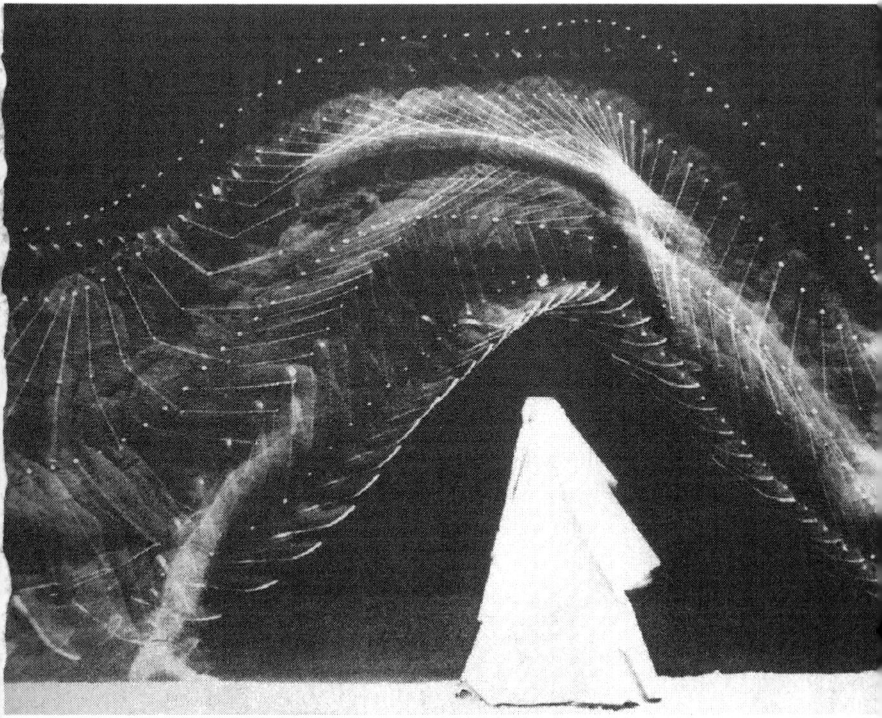

First published in 2014 by

# Schism prɛss

An imprint of Gobbet press

First edition
ISBN: 978-1503007161

Copyright © David Peak

Cover image: François-Auguste Biard
Cover design by GJS
Frontispiece: Étienne-Jules Marey

All rights reserved.
No part of this book may be reproduced or transmitted in any form or by any means, electronic or mechanical, including photocopying, recording, or by any information storage and retrieval system, without written consent of the publisher, except where permitted by law.

Printed in the USA.

*Only the inhuman thrived in out there in deep black.*

—*Laird Barron*

*The Spectacle of the Void*

David Peak

SC‡iSM

Contents

Part One: Toward a Horror Reality            11

Part Two: The Spectacle                      35

Part Three: The Void                         57

Part Four: Black Seas of Infinity            81

Notes                                        97

*The Spectacle of the Void*

# Part One: Toward a Horror Reality

> But the most normal solution, commonplace and public at the same time, communicable, shareable, is and will be the narrative. Narrative as the recounting of suffering: fear, disgust, and abjection crying out, they quiet down, concatenated into a story.
>
> –Julia Kristeva

1.1: The Narrative of Horror

The fundamental problem of human existence is rooted in an inherent inability to communicate. That's not to say that people are unable to talk to one another. In fact, people say a great deal to one another throughout any given day, much of it meaningless and instantly forgotten. It's only when the *meaning* of our words—the desperation of being *understood* by another—is made the locus of our communication, that the problems inherent to communication become impossible to ignore: wars are waged between governing bodies over conflicting intentions (*we know what's best for everyone, trust us*); murders occur over simple misunderstandings, wounded pride, and bruised egos (*you don't know me, how dare you*); a once-safe, nurturing relationship is torn apart by the need of lovers to be both heard and understood (*this is who I am, this is how I feel*). This is the dilemma of being human: believing that something needs to be communicated—a feeling, a thought, an urgent message—and not being able to communicate it; or, having made an attempt at communication and ultimately failing, causing irreparable harm.

In his book *Persuasion and Rhetoric*, Carlo Michelstaedter argues that language is merely determined by the senses, that any entity not "entirely at one with itself and the world,"[1] and therefore lacking what Michelstaedter refers to as "persuasion," is only able to use language as a means of maintaining a fear of death—hidden yet constant. "Having nothing and able to give nothing," he writes, "[men] let themselves sink into words that feign communication, because none of them can make his world be the world of the others; they feign words containing the absolute world, and with words they nourish their boredom, making for themselves a poultice for the pain; with words they show what they do not know and what they need in order to soothe the pain or make themselves numb to it."[2] This "poultice for the pain" is what Michelstaedter refers to as "rhetoric," or the "endless series of deceptions by which we try to convince ourselves and each other that we are persuaded . . ."[3]

The creation of narrative, then, like Michelstaedter's concept of rhetoric, has served to organize such deceptions into compelling, easily understood, and digestible language. What we consider "horror" fiction arises from this inability to communicate and is exemplified through two distinct types of narrative: 1) the narrative of the person with something to say that cannot be said (an inarticulate lucidity); and 2) the narrative of the person who is able to articulate their thoughts and feelings but still unable to make sense of their reality (an articulate confusion).

An excellent example of the former is Brian Evenson's short story "Mudder Tongue."

"Mudder Tongue" is the story of Hecker, a teacher and father, whose ability to communicate breaks down on a fundamental level; his words begin substituting themselves for each other, despite his thoughts remaining lucid. "Now, he *heard* himself say the wrong word, knew it to be wrong even while he was saying it, but was powerless to correct it. There was something seriously wrong with him, something broken. He could grasp that, but could not understand where it was taking him."[4] The horror that arises here is the dread of communication, the meaninglessness of all interactions and the anxiety that will ultimately result in failure and perhaps mistrust. "But no, he thought, the way people looked at him already, it was more than he could bear, and if it came tinged with pity, he would no longer feel human. Better to keep it to himself, hold it to himself as long as possible. And then he would still be, at least in part, human."[5]

Much like Lavinia, who had her tongue cut out so she could not identify her rapists, Hecker is able to release his inner struggle through the act of writing. Though this initially seems to work—it is only a temporary solution. Soon enough, Hecker has fallen deep within himself. He leaves his job and takes to bed, where he is visited by a doctor who decides to perform a series of tests. "A few days later, waiting for the results of the tests, he began to panic. *First*, he thought, *I will lose all language, then I will lose control of my body, then I will die.*"[6] It's this loss of language that convinces Hecker that he must kill himself, to flee his pain and become something other than human.

Conversely, there is the "articulate confusion" of Elisabeth in Jean Rollin's 1980 film *The Night of the Hunted*. The film opens with a man, Robert, driving down a deserted highway on a rainy night, the darkness solid beyond the pale yellow of his headlights. Suddenly, a woman in a thin, white nightgown leaps out into the road, her blank face betraying both shock and confusion. After chasing her down and confronting her, Robert discovers that although Elisabeth doesn't know where she's running from, she doesn't want to go back; although she doesn't know who she's running from, she doesn't want them to find her. Robert takes her home, where he quickly deduces that she's suffering from a kind of amnesia. "I don't know anything anymore," she says. "My mind is completely blank. You said that I was on the road, that I was running. I can't remember that. You just told me that you took me in your car. I can't remember that either. I can't remember anything that happened before I came in here." Despite her inability to grasp anything other than the current moment, Elisabeth is still able to fully articulate her confusion; her language has not failed her. "It's as if I'm searching for so many things that happened to me a long time ago. . . . I can't retrieve them. Just vague images, so far away."

*The Night of the Hunted* asks powerful questions about identity and the creation of reality through consciousness, the way we lie to ourselves in order to feel comfortable with what we see and what we know—or, in the words of one character, constructing a memory with the belief that reality reflects some sort of personal truth: "even if it's false, it's true." Ultimately, everything we see and know and think is—and has to be—the truth. Such is the illusion of persuasion. Michelstaedter: "Thus does what lives persuade itself that whatever life it lives is life."[7]

As the film progresses, it's revealed that Elisabeth has escaped from a prison hidden within a banal glass-and-steel office building referred to as the "black tower," where she is a patient of the deranged, Himmler-esque Dr. Francis and his twisted assistant, Solange. The black tower is filled with others who have lost their identities—the very memories that made them who they once were—and who remain haunted by vague impressions of their pasts. The patients wander the clinical interiors of the tower aimlessly, occasionally engaging in articulate conversations about their confusion, even creating elaborate fantasies of what memories their pasts may have contained.

Realizing Hecker's fears of losing bodily control in "Mudder Tongue," the patients of the black tower are slowly succumbing to what can only be described as a physical confusion, becoming, as one character phrases it, "clumsy." "I can feel myself going now," Elisabeth says toward the end of the film. "My mind is emptying. It's closing." Echoing Hecker's ultimate resolution to commit suicide, the patients resort to horrific acts of violence—in this case seemingly triggered by sexual arousal—both done unto others and their selves. In a way, it seems to be their only release, the only way that they can communicate the basest element of their humanity: savagery.

Since Lovecraft, horror has increasingly been concerned with the cosmic paralysis of humanity. This paralysis is caused by the realization that the underlying problem with communication is the dilemma of understanding our place, as humans, in the universe—that incalculably large void which envelopes us all. How can we begin to understand what this means in terms of instilling horror? In his landmark text, *Matter and Memory*, Henri Bergson frequently references the human mind, able to comprehend its place in the universe, as being privileged with consciousness. Alternately, the more recent philosophical tendency of speculative realism attempts to overcome philosophies of access, or philosophies such as Bergson's, that privilege human consciousness over other entities. The result of this contradiction, this overlap in two very different beliefs, is what we will refer to as *strangeness*. How can we possibly think past our own privilege as human beings, a privilege I am exercising with the very act of this writing? That you, in turn, are exercising by reading what I've written? The argument here is for a post-communication plane of thought—for thinking without language. This would be the existence of total horror: existence "understood" through the seemingly contradictory filters of an inarticulate lucidity and an articulate confusion. As Nicola Masciandaro writes, "That is what the world is (the result of a confusion between the world and a statement about the world)."[8] There is the world and there are our statements about the world—our rhetoric—all of which are different. Correlation of consciousness and language is inherently flawed and results only in failed communication and a reinforced sense of isolation. Our attempts at letting others know the strangeness of *how we feel* is not so much different from the message of the drowning man in a vast ocean, his attempts at communicating his mortal peril perhaps witnessed only by the shadowy shapes beneath the waves circling their prey, interpreting the man's flailing arms and thrashing legs as something wholly different from their intended meaning. What if those great predators of the deep believe the man is waving them over, offering his body as sustenance?

Bergson sought to "affirm the reality of spirit" with *Matter and Memory*, and speculative realism, at the risk of being reductive, proposes an alliance between metaphysics and empirical evidence. Why then are these two disparate bodies of thought being used for comparative purposes? As philosopher Graham Harman writes, "If there is one feature that unites the great works of philosophy, it is surely their inability to be fully assimilated, or their tendency to become such a given that we are blinded to their strangeness."[9] This is the reality of the world we are thrown into, the life we can only understand as life. Religion and science are often spoken of in the same sentence, without irony, as two sides of the same coin, equal threads in the argument over the meaning of existence, one contaminating the other. Sometimes, this can provide the basis for effective horror, such as in John Carpenter's film *Prince of Darkness*, which we discuss at length later on. Other times, this contamination results in a breakdown of communication that then leads to carnage and chaos. It is perhaps impossible to conceive of a consciousness in the modern world that *isn't* composed of contaminated or contradictory communication—the *strangeness* we are blind to, the *confusion* we cannot articulate. After all, it has been this way for thousands of years and will remain this way long after we perish. This strangeness is an integral element of what makes horror *horrific*.

Yet the question remains: what do we mean by *the world*? In his book *In the Dust of This Planet*, Eugene Thacker writes that there are three ways of interpreting the world as we know it: 1) the *world-for-us*, or the world in which we live; 2) the *world-in-itself*, or the inaccessible world that we then turn into the *world-for-us*; and

3) the *world-without-us*, or the spectral and speculative world.[10] "In a sense," he writes, "the world-without-us allows us to think the world-in-itself [. . .] The world-in-itself may co-exist with the world-for-us—indeed the human being is defined by its impressive capacity for not recognizing this distinction. By contrast, the world-without-us cannot co-exist with the human world-for-us; the world-without-us is the subtraction of the human from the world."[11]

Perhaps the creation of a so-called horror reality can—or already has—occurred through our limited comprehension of the universe and an inability to communicate the strangeness of the world-without-us. Like Chambers's fictional play *The King in Yellow*, which compels its viewers—its witnesses—to commit horrific acts, the uncovering and swallowing of the horror reality gives way to an ever-apparent understanding of cosmic dread—and eventual acceptance of the horror beyond horrors: our very extinction.

1.2: Imagination and Memory

Imagine a brain in outer space, floating motionless, surrounded by the black seas of infinity. The brain develops an eye, which turns to its surroundings, attempting to make sense of the empty black space, interpreting the light of the surrounding stars, the possible meaning of that light. The thoughts manifest a planet, a glowing orb swirling with milky clouds—its colors radiant. The planet is swarming with the world—the world-for-us—its finer details invisible from a great distance. The world comes together; a great amount of blood is shed over conflicts forgotten by time, and the colors of the glowing orb begin to change, to sour; the world breaks apart. The world-for-us, suddenly faced with the possibility of the world-without-us, looks beyond the known and toward the unknown, thus creating the otherworldly. This act of creation results in a great fear of the unknown, or the infinite black space that seems to endlessly push in from beyond. The brain cannot fathom the otherworldly and remains unaware of its own disappearance, slipping into those blackest folds between distant stars. The world then fills this void and visualizes the otherworldly as a brain in outer space, floating motionless, surrounded by the black seas of infinity.

Bergson writes: "Here I am in the presence of images, in the vaguest sense of the word, images perceived when my senses are opened to them, unperceived when they are closed. All these images act and react upon one another in all their elementary parts according to constant laws which I call laws of nature, and, as a perfect knowledge of these laws would probably allow us to calculate and to foresee what will happen in each of these images, the future of the images must be contained in their present and will add to them nothing new."[12]

Here, Bergson is talking about imagination—the calculation of foresight—or the literal act of seeing an image in relation to our physical being, how we might potentially interact with it, affect it, altering its reality as well as our own. This is similar to the basic narrative device of answering "what happens next," of *seeing things through*. Of the five senses, the visual sense is the most closely related to narrative, or the idea that, as Bergson explains, once our senses are exposed to images, our imagination will automatically envision the future of those images. In this way, image is central to the creation of narrative, by which I mean that, when generating language for the purpose of communication, image comes first, language second. This is an important concept in the creation of rhetoric—specifically the narrative of horror—which is ultimately rooted in the consciousness of body and the body's relation to both perceived and unperceived images, or the imagining of how reality may be acted upon by *the worst to come*. Again, Bergson: "The objects which surround my body reflect its possible action upon them."[13] It is impossible to separate our corporeal reality from the way in which we perceive images. All perception, in some way, relates to the consciousness of body.

The narrative of horror is composed of what we'll refer to as "meaningful" language, or language that emerges from the synesthesia of image and perception. It is important to also define the way we will be using the word "synesthesia." If meaningful language is composed of both image and perception in relation to the body, this then results in language that, when received by the listener/reader, creates an imaginative, sensory response; it is the language that ignites the senses, the language that is digested through the body as a way of relating to what is being told. Thus, imagination is in full force when our senses are opened to images and their representation through language.

As can be inferred from the title of Bergson's *Matter and Memory*, imagination isn't just about the way we take in images, but also how those images are later called upon, eventually composing the fabric of what we refer to as memory, which is defined by Bergson as "the survival of past images, [which] must constantly mingle with our perception of the present and may even take its place."[14]

In Georges Bataille's sensational novel *Story of the Eye*, a crucial moment occurs when the narrator attends a bullfight in Madrid, accompanied by his lover, Simone, and their mutual acquaintance, Sir Edmond. The bullfighter they are interested in watching, Granero, is considered one of the two best matadors in Spain. While facing off against the fourth bull of the afternoon, Granero is wedged against the balustrade and gored through the head, an injury which leaves his right eyeball dangling from its socket. This moment is paralleled the next day, when the trio visits the church of Don Juan in Seville. Here, Simone enters a tabernacle and confesses to the priest, Don Aminado. After admitting to Don Aminado that she has been masturbating during her confession, Simone accuses the priest of doing the same, pulling him out of the tabernacle and stripping him of his cassock.

What follows is degradation at its most absurd: the narrator and Sir Edmond watch "in [a] stupor" as Simone begins sucking off the priest; then the three of them strip him down; they piss on him, humiliate him, and eventually beat him with the chalice used to hold the church's white wine. Mercifully, Don Aminado is brought to orgasm. Afterward, the priest is dejected, ashamed, and begins insulting his aggressors. A brief argument results in Don Aminado being bound and gagged. "You are going to have the pleasure of being martyred while fucking this girl," Sir Edmond says. While straddling the priest, inserting him into herself, Simone chokes him to death and receives the ejaculate of his death throes. Freshly killed, the priest's eyes remain open, and a fly lands on one of his exposed eyeballs. Simone demands the priest's eye be removed from his head. Using scissors, Sir Edmond obliges her request, handing over the "small whitish eyeball in a hand reddened with blood."[15] Simone takes the eyeball and promptly inserts it into her ass.

Later, in a note that almost reads like a confession, Bataille explains the inspiration for this scene. Granero, apparently, was a real bullfighter whom Bataille had actually witnessed being injured. While writing the scene of Don Aminado's mutilation in the vestry, Bataille suddenly became aware of the parallel between the two moments. "I was merely transferring, to a different person, an image that had most likely led a very profound life. If I devised the business about snipping out the priest's eye, it was because I had seen a bull's horn tear out a matador's eye. Thus, precisely the two images that probably most upset me had sprung from the darkest corner of my memory—and in a scarcely recognizable shape . . ."[16] In the same explanation, Bataille writes that this "coincidence" brought out the meaning of what he wrote, allowing him to fully see the memory in his imagination and express it with meaningful language. In other words, his memory contained images of a bodily trauma that remained hidden away in the recesses of his consciousness until the act of writing, or the act of summoning language to communicate to readers, released them. The fact that Bataille refers to these images of trauma as those "that probably most upset me" is significant. It probably isn't a stretch to claim that he was haunted by the image of Granero's eyeball—that image forever lurking in the "darkest corner" of his memory—throughout his life. Many writers of horror fiction talk of these sort of "hauntings" manifesting themselves in their writing, as if the act of writing were to exorcise such demons, or purge oneself of the gaping wounds caused by bodily trauma.

This leads us to the idea of *the mind's eye*, or the mechanism with which human consciousness interprets images as language. All of the calculations of foresight, as mentioned earlier, are accomplished through the mind's eye, which we should think of as the brain of the brain, sorting through an endless stream of signs and symbols and interpreting those signs and symbols as received knowledge—the very building blocks of our reality. The mind's eye, then, is an extension of our privilege as beings with consciousness—an indispensable aspect of our ability to communicate or craft language—but it is also a burden, frequently using those building blocks of reality to erect the walls of a prison. Again, Bergson: "It is true that an image may *be* without *being perceived*—it may be present without being represented—and the distance between these two terms, presence and representation, seems just to measure the interval between matter itself and our conscious perception of matter."[17] All of existence is incarcerated in our perceptions of matter, or what Bergson often refers to as the "aggregate of images."

Perhaps the text most responsible for instigating the conversation around speculative realism is Quentin Meillassoux's *After Finitude*. In it, Meillassoux articulates a key problem in philosophy, namely to "achieve what modern philosophy has been telling us for the past two centuries is impossibility itself: to get out of ourselves, to grasp the in-itself, to know what is, whether we are or not."[18] One of Meillassoux's central concerns is furthering philosophical thought beyond what is frequently referred to by speculative realists as correlationism, or the idea popularized by Kant that our existence is limited to the correlation of thinking and being. This initially seems to improve upon Bergson's idea that an image may be present without being represented, which makes perfect sense on its own, but fails to take into account leaps of imagination beyond memory, or how we could possibly represent images that are not present, either in discernible reality or the fabric of our memory—the images of horror narrative's infatuation with not only the body but also the *beyond* (the unknowable). With this in mind, it is fair to say then that to be human is to be both imprisoned in our limited comprehension of the universe and "privileged" with the burden of consciousness. Being human with an inescapable corporeal reality and simultaneously possessing consciousness, in and of itself, creates an inescapable state of horror. And considering the close relationship of horror to flight, or the urge to escape, it is impossible to consider being without the constant need for an exit. Levinas: "Escape is the need to get out of oneself, that is, *to break that most radical and unalterably binding of chains, the fact that the I [moi] is oneself [soi même]*."[19] And then, "It is being itself or the 'one-self' from which escape flees, and in no wise being's limitation. In escape the I flees itself, not in opposition to the infinity of what it is not or of what it will not become, but rather due to the very fact that it is or that it becomes."[20]

If Bergson's thinking—or really the act of following any single philosophical system as "absolute truth"—provides the terror of being incarcerated within consciousness, then the ideas posited by speculative realism—and more specifically *After Finitude*—are the terror of the lifelong prisoner suddenly being told he's being released, having freedom thrown upon him, and the anxiety of knowing he'll soon be thrown into a world of unrecognizable signs and the unknowable shadows of unfriendly dimensions.

1.3: Extra-dimensionality

Roman Polanski's 1965 film *Repulsion* opens with the image of an eye. The eye remains attentive for the duration of the opening credits, moving slightly, taking in new information, reacting, the black pupil adjusting minutely to perceived changes in light. The percussion-heavy score sounds suspiciously like a heartbeat, a whining drone like the signal of an EKG—alerting the attentive viewer to body consciousness. When the credits have finished rolling, we are presented with a medium shot of the astoundingly beautiful Carol, a quiet and soft-spoken beautician who lives with her sister. The first few scenes clearly demonstrate that Carol is a young and damaged woman who suffers from compulsive behaviors and sexual phobias. These behaviors and phobias will eventually, as the film progresses, cause her to descend into paranoia, madness, and, ultimately, in a fit of terrified disorientation, commit multiple murders.

The vast majority of the scenes in *Repulsion* take place within the confines of Carol's apartment, its rooms and hallways composed of—and defined by—the ordered rigidity of vertical and horizontal lines. The scenes that take place outdoors are often populated with leering faces, unfinished construction projects, car accidents, etc.—all symbols of the inherent danger, or chaos, of public spaces. Within the apartment, Polanski goes to great lengths to establish the spatial relations of each room, often framing shots with the hard lines of kitchen counters and shelves, or through doorways and peepholes. Likewise, various intermittent sounds can often be heard on the soundtrack—the ticking of an alarm clock, a leaking faucet, bells chiming—that regulate the passage of time, as if anchoring temporality with spatial metaphors. Daily life within the defined and understood dimensions of the apartment is enclosed, established and, seemingly well-ordered.

Nearly halfway through the film, Carol is left alone in the apartment when her sister, accompanied by her boyfriend, leaves for the weekend. A large fracture suddenly splits the wall around an air vent—in this case a literal crack in Carol's perceived reality or understanding of safety. More invasions from beyond soon follow: images of men in mirrors, the sounds of footsteps in the hallway, nighttime visits from imagined—or perhaps remembered?—rapists. In her gradual mental unraveling, Carol leaves out a skinned and uncooked rabbit, its increasingly decayed flesh signifying, perhaps, her mental state.

In the film's central scene, Carol sits on the couch in the living room, staring at a family photo featuring herself as a child. The entire wall suddenly cracks open. Carol flees into the hallway and braces herself with her hand against the wall. As she removes her hand, she sees that she's left behind an indent of her fingertips, as if the wall were composed of wet clay. The ring of the doorbell—this time sounding as if it were coming from a great distance—steals away her attention. Through the peephole, Carol sees Colin, a hopeless romantic who has developed something of an obsession with Carol's closed-off beauty. Carol refuses to let Colin in, so he forces his way in. As soon as he turns his back to her—in this case to shut the door on the prying eyes of an elderly neighbor—Carol bludgeons Colin with a candlestick. Only the sight of blood running over Colin's ear shakes Carol from her stupor. In a panic, she submerges Colin's body in the bathtub.

At this point, Carol's reality has become a horror reality. For the remainder of *Repulsion*, there is no longer any clear passage of time. All of the food that has been left out swarms with flies. Scenes switch abruptly from day to night. In one particularly breathtaking scene, Carol leaves the confines of her room and enters the hallway, the dimensions of which now seem utterly distorted, as if the hallway itself were longer than the apartment that contains it. As Carol passes the door leading into the living room, she looks inside, only to see that the room is now cavernous—the walls of reality have literally fallen away to an extra-dimensionality. Likewise, the bathroom has elongated into something like a cellar, or, considering that Colin's body is still in the tub, perhaps a tomb. Not only are the cracks on the wall more prevalent than before, they now seem to be sprouting groping hands, literal invasions from beyond. The penultimate horror arrives as Carol lies paralyzed in her bed at night, perhaps fearing yet another nighttime visit, yet another remembrance of sexual trauma, as the ceiling of her room literally falls down upon her.

*Repulsion* ends on a close-up of the family photo featuring Carol as a child, the image of herself separated or zoned in by shadows, followed by a parallel image to the opening of the film—an eye—as it fills the frame, this time frozen wide open. In this closing shot, the camera zooms in on the image of Carol's childhood eye until the image distorts, breaking down into something unrecognizable, an eye frozen open in a warped perception, an inarticulate lucidity, suggesting the permanency of madness.

Concerned with similar themes of madness and the breakdown of spatial relations, J. G. Ballard wrote of a man driven to madness by perceptions of interiority in his story "The Enormous Space": "By shutting out the world my mind may have drifted into a realm without yardsticks or sense of scale. For so many years I have longed for an empty world, and may have unwittingly constructed it within this house. Time and space have rushed in to fill the vacuum that I have created."[21] The details of a dark space are defined by the light cast within it; without that light, there could be *anything* lurking around—or *nothing at all*. No one has ever seen the center of the earth, though surely it exists. I recognize the person in the mirror as a reflection of myself, though there is always the possibility that each mirror is a window looking out upon someone else whose movements and appearance merely match mine. These are the extra-dimensional "illusions" of the horror reality, the spaces "from beyond" that lend reality the dread of the horrific, the inklings of a world which, as Ballard writes, "came to claim me." Michelstaedter: "When the light dims, the image of dear things—the screen veiling the external obscurity—becomes more tenuous, and the invisible grows visible; when the weave of illusion thins, disintegrates, tears asunder, then men, *made impotent*, feel themselves in the sway of what is *outside their power, of what they do not know: they fear without knowing what they fear.*"[22]

In *After Finitude*, Meillassoux writes that the world itself has no "physical limits." What we perceive as limits are in actuality an illusion in the same sense that a two-dimensional photograph, laid flat on a table, could seemingly be perceived as having depth when seen from above. The illusion is the representation of space within space, the angles of interiority as perceived by the mind's eye processing them. Again, Ballard: "But already the walls of this once tiny room constitute a universe of their own. The ceiling is so distant that clouds might form below it."[23] Understanding space—the dimensions of interiors, the dimensions of the-world-as-we-know-it, and the vacuum that seeks only to fill that space—is how we determine our reality. Anything beyond that understanding is the horror reality.

Lovecraft wrote of extra-dimensionality often. For instance, in "The Call of Cthulhu," the storyteller Johansen describes the disappearance of a sailor named Parker who was "swallowed up by an angle of masonry which shouldn't have been there; an angle which was acute, but behaved as if it were obtuse."[24] Or in "The Colour Out of Space," which begins with the following two sentences: "West of Arkham the hills rise wild, and there are valleys with deep woods that no axe has ever cut. There are dark narrow glens where the trees slope fantastically, and where thin brooklets trickle without ever having caught the glint of sunlight."[25] Or "The Dreams in the Witch House," in which a student named Gilman takes a room in an ancient house whose interiors seem to obey the laws of a distinctly non-Euclidean geometry. "As time wore along, his absorption in the irregular wall and ceiling of his room increased; for he began to read into the odd angles a mathematical significance which seemed to offer vague clues regarding their purpose. . . . His interest gradually veered away from the unplumbed voids beyond the slanting surfaces, since it now appeared that the purpose of those surfaces concerned the side he was already on."[26] In "From Beyond," Crawford Tillinghast claims to have built a machine that will "overleap time, space, and dimensions, and without bodily motion peer to the bottom of creation."[27] And then, of course, there is "At the Mountains of Madness," Lovecraft's masterpiece, which details the Arctic expedition of geologist William Dyer, whose team discovers "a Cyclopean city of no architecture known to man or to human imagination, with vast aggregations of night-black masonry embodying monstrous perversions of geometrical laws and attaining the most grotesque extremes of sinister bizarrerie."[28]

Regarding the extra-dimensionality of Lovecraft's writing, Michel Houellebecq writes, "H. P. Lovecraft's architecture, like that of great cathedrals, like that of Hindu temples, is much more than a three-dimensional mathematical puzzle. It is entirely imbued with an essential dramaturgy that gives its meaning to the edifice. That dramatizes the very smallest spaces, that uses the conjoint resources of the various plastic arts, that annexes the magic play of light to its own ends. It is *living* architecture because at its foundation lies a living and emotional concept of the world."[29]

Houellebecq here offers a particularly interesting phrase—"the magic play of light"—that we should briefly discuss further. Magic, of course, is inextricably linked to superstition, or *illusions*, a word we have previously employed to help us understand what we mean by extra-dimensionality, which could otherwise be defined as the human control—or the perceived human control—of supernatural forces. In this sense, the horror of extra-dimensionality occurs when human consciousness interferes with supernatural forces beyond our comprehension. It is the horror of unknown interiors, the failure of our geometry, and the disruption or contamination of natural order—all things that are impossible to communicate.

"So long as we believe that there must be a reason why what is, is the way it is," Meillassoux writes, "we will continue to fuel superstition, which is to say, the belief that there is an ineffable reason underlying all things. Since we will never be able to discover or understand such a reason, all we can do is believe in it."[30] Here, meaningful language arises once more, of the synesthesia of language and image—the "living architecture" of the body itself, the prison of our consciousness able to conceive of but never fully understand extra-dimensionality.

1.4: A New Dark Age

George J. Sieg writes, "Independently of, yet inclusive of, both *self* and *other*, Horror pervades consciousness which is conscious of itself: to observe someone sufficiently horrified is horrific. To observe a horrific other—a 'monster'—is horrific. Yet to observe oneself horrified is just as horrific, if not more. Thus, Horror also maintains the fascinating quality of being self-renewing, for while awe and wonder may both collapse under sufficiently detached rational observation, Horror only seems to increase the more it is contemplated."[31]

*Horror pervades consciousness which is conscious of itself.* We are taught that as time moves forward, as it unfailingly will, humans will continue to evolve—despite the likelihood of evolution's trajectory resembling the shape of a circle—to accept new discoveries of knowledge and logical thinking in an effort to afford our lives greater meaning. The Dark Ages were referred to as such because they were a time of darkness and decay. Subsequent historical periods, such as the appropriately titled Age of Enlightenment, were focused wholly around the battle between reason and religion—that familiar dilemma of understanding our place, as humans, in the universe—and always with the idea that we were moving away from darkness, toward light: the inarguable reason and logic of scientific thinking. Relating this idea to the consuming, pervasive nature of horror, Arthur Machen wrote in his novella *The Terror*:

> As Lewis glanced down over the terraces he saw that the tall pine tree was no longer there. In its place there rose above the ilexes what might have been a greater ilex; there was the blackness of a dense growth of foliage rising like a broad and far-spreading and rounded cloud over the lesser trees.
>
> Here, then was a sight wholly incredible, impossible. It is doubtful whether the process of the human mind in such a case has ever been analyzed and registered; it is doubtful it ever can be registered. It is hardly fair to bring in the mathematician, since he deals with absolute truth (so far as mortality can conceive absolute truth); but how would a mathematician feel if he were suddenly confronted with a two-sided triangle; I suppose he would instantly become a raging madman; and Lewis, staring wide-eyed and wild-eyed at a dark and spreading tree which his own experience informed him was not there, felt for an instant that shock which should affront us all when we first realize the

> intolerable antinomy of Achilles and the Tortoise."[32]

Earlier, we mentioned the cross-contamination of religion and science as equal elements of the argument over the meaning of existence, the schism that leads to the creation of strangeness, and briefly mentioned John Carpenter's *Prince of Darkness*, the second entry in Carpenter's "Apocalypse Trilogy," preceded by *The Thing* in 1982 and followed by *In the Mouth of Madness* in 1995.

*Prince of Darkness*, more than anything else, is an ambitious film—within the genre of horror or otherwise—in that it attempts to articulate the battle between good and evil through scientific discourse. The general thesis being: if there is a god willing the behavior of every sub-atomic particle in existence, including our biological makeup, and if every particle has an anti-particle, a negative side or "mirror-image," then logic dictates that an anti-god exists within the order of our universe, imprisoned within the realm of anti-matter. In this case, the extra-dimensionality of the horror to be found in *Prince of Darkness* is literally waiting on the other side of the mirror.

The corporeal embodiment of the son of the Anti-Christ is buried in a container "eons ago" and maintained under vow of silence by a forgotten religious sect known as the Brotherhood of Sleep. The priest who discovers this secret, Father Loomis, then enlists the help of theoretical physicist Professor Howard Birack and his team of graduate students to investigate, perhaps knowing that their faith in facticity, rather than religion, is the only means of grasping the evil at hand. "It's your disbelief that powers him," Father Loomis says to Birack. "Your stubborn faith . . . in common sense that allows his deception."

Again, Meillassoux is helpful here. "So long as we construe facticity as a limit for thought, we will abandon whatever lies beyond this limit to the rule of piety. Thus, in order to interrupt this see-sawing between metaphysics and fideism, we must transform our perspective on unreason, stop construing it as the form of our deficient grasp of the world and turn it into the veridical content of this world as such—we must project unreason into things themselves, and discover in our grasp of facticity the veritable *intellectual intuition* of the absolute."[33]

Compare this thinking, then, to Professor Birack's lecture on metaphysics at the beginning of the film: "Let's talk about our beliefs and what we can learn about them. We believe nature is solid and time a constant. Matter has substance and time a direction. There is truth in flesh and the solid ground. The wind may be invisible but it's real. Smoke, fire, water, light—they're different not as to stone nor steel, but they're tangible. And we assume time has an arrow, because it is as a clock. One second is one second for everyone. Cause precedes effect. Fruit rots, water flows downstream. We're born, we age, we die. The reverse never happens."

Meillassoux is essentially arguing for the transformation of "our perspective on unreason," a line of reasoning echoed by Professor Birack as he continues his lecture: "Our logic collapses on the sub-atomic level into ghosts and shadows." And then, "While order does exist in the universe, it is not at all what we had in mind."

As the film progresses, the scientists learn that the liquid inside the canister is producing data in the form of differential equations, which, once decoded, reveal that the liquid is in fact the corporeal embodiment of the son of the Anti-Christ—the being capable of flooding the world-in-itself with the world-without-us. Day turns to night as increasingly bizarre, if not outright impossible events take place: a slimy mass of earthworms writhes over the vertical surface of a window; the fluid from the canister spills upward and pools on the ceiling. One of the scientists sums all of this strangeness up rather nicely when he says, "Nothing . . . anywhere ever is supposed to be able to do what it is doing." As if to further prove this point, the liquid within the container begins exhibiting signs of sentience—of consciousness itself—using psychokinesis to literally reach out and interact with and alter its surrounding reality. The horror here is that something from an extra-dimensional reality could disrupt what Meillassoux terms "the principle of the uniformity of nature," a law that states that "given the same initial conditions, the same results invariably follow."[34]

*Prince of Darkness* shines a brilliant light on the ways in which an inarticulate confusion leads to a horror reality. The scientists in Carpenter's film do their best to articulate the horror disrupting the principle of the uniformity of nature, to relate their findings through the language of science, to fight their superstitions at all costs. Ultimately, those who survive the confrontation with evil are those who accept their reality as being replaced with a horror reality, embracing the impossible as the new uniformity of nature. In this sense, coming to understand the horror reality is the acceptance of a return to the contemplative consciousness of the unknown. Those who survive their encounter with the unknowable no longer conceal their true condition from themselves and each other, having been successfully persuaded to accept illusion as reality. In other words, they emerge freed of the illusion of rhetoric.

This idea was perhaps expressed most clearly by Lovecraft in the famous first paragraph of his story "The Call of Cthulhu," which, as well-known as it is, deserves to be repeated in full here: "The most merciful thing in the world, I think, is the inability of the human mind to correlate all its contents. We live on a placid island of ignorance in the midst of black seas of infinity, and it was not meant that we should voyage far. The sciences, each straining in its own direction, have hitherto harmed us little; but some day the piecing together of dissociated knowledge will open up such terrifying vistas of reality, and of our frightful position therein, that we shall either go mad from the revelation or flee the deadly light into the peace and safety of a new dark age."[35] Graham Harman writes in *Weird Realism: Lovecraft and Philosophy*: "Enlightened, rational humans scoff at all hidden or occult qualities, and other palpable evidence for their conclusions. In this way, enlightened humans are able to reject many of the gullible superstitions of the past. But by the same stroke, they also become over-intellectualized, which means that they are sadly mesmerized by the surface qualities of things. Only when these qualities go terribly awry . . . do we slowly become attuned to the fact that the fault-lines of the cosmos have been ruptured."[36]

If we have learned anything at all, we have learned that we know nothing. And so we continue moving forward through time, spilling our words in great heaps, trying and failing again and again to let others know *what it really means* to be alive, to express our fear, our disgust, and our abjection. Certainly I'm as guilty of that as anyone else who saw fit to set words to paper—and that guilt hangs heavy.

Crying out, we quiet down.

# Part Two: The Spectacle

> No one who has experienced the need to look at the same time as the longing to go beyond mere looking will find it easy to imagine how clearly and definitely these two processes coexist . . .
>
> –Friedrich Nietzsche

> Eyes preoccupied with watching do not see.
>
> –Carlo Michelstaedter

2.1: The Shadows on the Wall

Like Bataille and his image of the bullfighter's eyeball, the horror image—the image of trauma—haunts the darkest corners of our memory. That which has been seen cannot be unseen, and that which remains unseen remains limited to the realm of speculation. If, as Lovecraft said in his essay "Supernatural Horror in Literature," fear is the "oldest and strongest emotion of mankind," then can we not assume that the prisoners in Plato's cave spent a great deal of their time haunted by the shapes of the shadows on the wall? How often must the fingers of those flickering shadows have appeared as slithering serpents? If these prisoners truly had no understanding of life beyond their own imprisonment—or perhaps even no *conception* of their imprisonment—then we can only imagine what those fears were, what strange stories unfolded beneath the hiss and crackle of those blackening flames. This is not unlike how we continually create and consume images of violence and horror, whether in writing or films. Much like the vampire—monster incarnate, death itself—creating more death by feeding on the living, we, as human beings, have an unbearable need to witness the suffering of others as a way of affirming our very existence. To put it another way, we feed on images of death and suffering in order to feel alive. Fear, after all, is a product of our senses, a warning induced by perceived threat. It is a necessary aspect for the survival of our—and perhaps all—species. Looking deeper, we can differentiate between two distinct ways in which fear directly affects action. If we know why we're scared we can subsequently articulate that fear to others. Hopefully they'll understand our situation and offer to help in some way. In this sense, fear drives us to seek company. Other times, however, fear exists as nothing more than vague dread or anxiety. The threat isn't so much perceived as it is lurking in the periphery. This sort of fear is isolating and drives us deeper within the self.

In *The Birth of Tragedy*, Nietzsche created a distinction between two kinds of art: 1) the Dionysian (the actual experience of emotions and instincts); and 2) the Apollonian (critical distance, separating man from those emotions).

"The Greeks," he wrote, "knew and felt the fears and horrors of existence: in order to be able to live at all they had to interpose the radiant dream-birth of the Olympians between themselves and those horrors."[37] By creating tragedy, the Greeks were able to affirm life beneath these gods, often in celebration of those gods. And then: "With sublime gestures [Apollo] reveals to us how the whole world of torment is necessary so that the individual can create the redeeming vision, and then, immersed in contemplation of it, sit peacefully in his tossing boat amid the waves."[38] Apollo was the god of, among other things, music and poetry. He was an oracle, a healer—a protector of man from evil. Thus it makes sense for the Greeks to view tragedy as something that ultimately demonstrates the good in life, that the "highest dignity lies at the meanings of art."[39] In this sense, *The*

*Birth of Tragedy* describes why we're drawn to works of dramatic representation that deal with violence, suffering and horrible ends, and ultimately claims that the transcendence offered by such sights is capable of affirming the spirit of man.

It's only in the last few centuries that a greater importance has been placed on the *horrific* rather than the *tragic*, perhaps most formatively in nineteenth- and twentieth-century ghost stories, which, according to Roger B. Salomon in his book *Mazes of the Serpent*, "represents both the deepening 'malaise' of 'theological doubt' and, ironically, some continuing commitment to 'spiritualism.'"[40] Essentially, as we move away from the idea of a spiritual existence—however slowly—and come to accept a material or realist existence, the world-for-us will only continue to descend into the horrific, the uncaring and barren; the human being will become more isolated in their misery, less willing to believe that suffering signals some meaning or higher purpose. This horror is then reflected in the art and culture we consume. Soon enough, a need develops—a return.

It goes much deeper than the ways in which we interpret art and culture, however, this need to look—to see what cannot be unseen. It is ingrained in the very nature of our being. As stated in the previous chapter, all thought is merely a perception of received or imagined images; this perception is then translated into language through the mind's eye. With this in mind, our need to look is merely an extension of attempting to articulate the strangeness of our reality. Take, for example, a man driving his car past the scene of a horrible wreck: the police and emergency medical technicians arrive; traffic slows down, funneled perhaps into a single lane; each driver is then waved past the scene of the disaster in a gloomy procession. When it's the man's turn to pass, he can't help but look at the grisly horror within the twisted metal. *At least it wasn't me*, he thinks, all-too-aware of the steering wheel in his hands, the way the engine's rumblings cause it to vibrate against his palms, the way that feeling radiates through the bones in his arms, pooling at the base of his neck. Once again, an awareness of body has been raised through glimpsing the inevitable *worst to come.*

So what does it mean when Nietzsche refers to the "longing to go beyond mere looking?" Essentially, he is referring to what he calls the "inner world of motives" existent within an image. "and yet we felt as though we were watching a symbol," he writes, "almost imagining we could divine its deepest meaning, and wishing to draw it aside like a curtain to glimpse the primordial image that lay behind."[41] Is there an inherent truth within any given image? Is there an origin to the images of our suffering? Does witnessing the end result of a terrible car wreck teach us anything about ourselves? Or is it merely a repulsive reminder that life is fragile and that cars are dangerous?

Thomas Ligotti writes, "Among other things, Nietzsche is famed as a promoter of human survival, just as long as enough of the survivors follow his lead as a *perverted pessimist*—one who has consecrated himself to loving life exactly because it is the worst thing imaginable, a sadomasochistic joyride through the twists and turns of being unto death. Nietzsche had no problem with human existence as a tragedy born of consciousness—parent of all horrors."[42] Ligotti's line of thinking here is particularly relevant to the idea of the horror reality—that, once hatched, horror pervades consciousness which is conscious of itself. It's difficult to read Ligotti's comment on Nietzsche's "loving life exactly because it is the worst thing imaginable" as anything other than mocking, yet he makes a worthwhile point: why should we look to the tragic—to *looking* itself—as a means of affirming our humanity? It could be argued that works of human creation, however "negative" in their outlook, are testaments to the human spirit in the sense that only lovers of life could harness the discipline and energy needed to create them. If you don't care about other humans, or even yourself, then why bother to better yourself through reading? Why bother to communicate your thoughts? By that logic, only lovers of life would feel the need to consume these creations as a means of learning something about the world-for-us. Of course, such optimistic reasoning is far from true. Creation is just as likely to arise from dread, just as likely to be aimed toward destruction. This, then, is what we mean when we refer to the concept of *the spectacle*—the insatiable need to view the suffering of others. Origins of spectacle, whether Dionysian (car wrecks, impulsive violence) or Apollonian (creations of art, compositions of language), each contain an inner-world of motives that imparts some new knowledge upon those who "look" at them. What that knowledge is, whether or not we find the light blinding, is impossible to predict, and entirely dependent on an unknowable myriad of factors—all of which can be said to form a single person's consciousness. But one thing is consistent in this concept of the spectacle: no matter what we believe to be the core tenets of our reality, we all feel the need to look at the same time as longing to go beyond mere looking.

Ligotti, writing under the moniker of Professor Nobody, takes this idea even further in his lecture "Sardonic Harmony," which ends with the following sentence: "Once and for all, let us speak the paradox aloud: 'We have been force-fed for so long the shudders of a thousand graveyards that at last, seeking a macabre redemption, a salvation by horror, we willingly consume the terrors of the tomb . . . and find them to our liking.'"[43]

As readers of horror narrative and viewers of the horror image, we are drawn both willingly and unwillingly—in tandem—to consume the spectacle. *At least it wasn't me*, we think, and yet, deep down inside we know that it *will be*. Some would argue that no one actually believes they will be visited by the worst to come because there is no way of correlating this knowledge with what we know, just as we are unable to conceive of a pain detached from the subject that feels it. We cannot *think* the unthinkable. Yet how often do we *see* it? This is the *spectacle*—the shadows on the wall—and we are unable to see these shadows for what they really are because our eyes are filled with darkness.

## 2.2: Lifting the Veil

With *The Birth of Tragedy*, Nietzsche ultimately attempted to explain that our lives are governed by unseen forces beyond our comprehension, that there is a world of inner motives hidden behind a veil we are oblivious to. Our valiant struggle to imagine the workings of the universe—*our* universe—is ultimately pointless; we will never be able to acknowledge the underlying truths of existence. All truth is beyond comprehension—and all comprehension is nothing more than skimming the surface of oceanic depths—so we must turn to art for revelations of truth and beauty. Therefore it is our fate, as humans, to accept a reality composed entirely of illusions. This is essentially an argument for a supernatural understanding of existence. Or, as Professor Nobody says in his lecture, "Pessimism and Supernatural Horror—Lecture One": "In transforming natural ordeals into supernatural ones, we find the strength to affirm and deny their horror simultaneously, to savor and suffer them at the same time."[44]

The roots of the supernatural in horror literature are often traced back to the idea of alternate worlds. In horror, these worlds do not simply exist alongside our own, like Nietzsche's world of inner motives, but actively *infringe* upon our own. This is something that Salomon explicitly states early on in *Mazes of the Serpent* when he says that horror is constituted by "scarcely veiled places that we cross into or that otherwise may intrude on our commonplace experience."[45] Like Nietzsche's unseen forces, the realms of horror are often understood only as the unthinkable or previously unimaginable, whether they originate through subterranean, inter-dimensional, or cosmological means—it isn't important. What matters is that this new reality shows us something we either don't want to see or, having seen, cannot correlate or comprehend. Salomon explains, "this alternate world, insofar as we might encounter it at all and survive, is one of dissolution and death."[46] How many horror stories feature a protagonist who lives a so-called normal life before being shown, stumbling upon, or crossing over into the world beyond the veil? An alternate world, once revealed, will either be something we cannot explain to others or even to ourselves; conversely, if we are somehow able to put what we have seen into words, no one will believe us. How could they? Either way, as is often the case in horror literature, the traveler beyond the veil is, to one degree or another, isolated from others by their new knowledge. They will be unable to return to the way things once were—or *appeared* to be.

Salomon goes on to say that "horror narrative always tells an old story in deliberate response to the newer stories."[47] In this sense, the veil is merely time passed, the currency of life spent, and not any sort of conventionally understood portal to a Lovecraftian beyond. Writer and editor of horror fiction, G. Winston Hyatt, elaborated on this idea in a personal communication to me saying that a state of horror can be created by "reaching back" into previous realities and "applying" them to current reality. This is a fascinating reinterpretation of "lifting the veil." In Hyatt's idea, exemplified by so much of horror fiction that dwells on hauntings from previous times—restless spirits, tainted grounds—the past reality takes on the significance of the horrific because we live in a comfortable present. Furthering this thought, Hyatt later wrote to me in an email: "The terrorized have little use for tales of terror." Horror, as a genre, exists because the experience of fear, when removed from an environment of immediate survival, is considered by many to be pleasurable. It is the vacuum seeking to fill the space created by perceived safety and comfort. Likewise, representations of the impossible are valued in a world that is all-too-real.

Joyce Carol Oates expressed similar thinking in her well-researched article on H. P. Lovecraft titled "The King of Weird." "To love the past," she writes, "to extol the past, to yearn in some way to inhabit the past is surely to misread the past, purposefully or otherwise; above all, it is to select from the past only those aspects that accommodate a self-protective and nourishing fantasy. What is 'past' tempts us to reconstruct a world rather like a walled city, finite and contained and in the most literal sense predictable."[48]

A horror reality, however, demands that horror already exists within us—or without us—by nature of our very consciousness; it is the very fabric of our memories and the projections of our imaginations. In that case, the portal to the *beyond* can only exist as the horror *within*, the constant give and take of looking while longing to go beyond mere looking. It is the letting of fears in an effort to assuage the strangeness of the world-without-us. This endless struggle leads to the consumption of fresh morbidity and anxiety, which, unpalatable as always, will be internalized, digested and manifested as new *spectacle*.

Think of it this way: there is a table in an empty room; let's say our conception of current reality is represented by the flat surface of a table, something we can understand concretely; the space below the table should be considered a past reality, something undefined yet undeniably existent; now lay a black cloth over the entire surface of the table, allowing its long edges to hang to the floor, thus containing the past reality and obscuring the current reality; this cloth, then, is the veil obscuring an alternate world, which should be considered the empty room itself—and anything beyond its walls should be considered the unthinkable. Now let's take this a step further: imagine a man trapped below this table, existent in a horror reality, his understanding of the room itself occluded by the black cloth; lying on his back, he is able to feel an understanding of the present (the underside of the table's surface) while inhabiting the space of his past (he is haunted by his memories); given some mechanism with which to puncture the underside of the table, the man creates a hole that tears through the black cloth, creating a portal through which to see into the room itself; when he presses his eye to the hole, whatever he sees there—the unknown beyond—will project either some manifestation of his hopes and wishes or his fears. Only, imagine the sheer horror the man would feel if, when looking through the hole, he catches a glimpse of another searching eye, perhaps his own, reflected in the surface of a mirror. As Nietzsche so famously wrote in *Beyond Good and Evil*, "When you gaze long into an abyss the abyss also gazes into you."[49] This is the *horror within*, the finding of oneself, the eternal return to the self and the inescapable prison of consciousness, in the searching of what lies beyond the veil.

Once more, we turn to the discomfiting teachings of Professor Nobody: "Just a little doubt slipped into the mind, a little trickle of suspicion in the bloodstream, and all those eyes of ours, one by one, open up to the world and see its horror."[50] The horror within is always the end result of turning to the spectacle, of being so bold as to lift the veil; it is the space occupied by our body or the space that exists in the chasms between accepted, remembered or imagined realities.

2.3: Viewership, Bearing Witness, and Guilt

Because film creates a language composed of images and signs, which are then interpreted by viewers as memory and imagination, it is a medium uniquely able to convey the guilt inherent to viewership—of capturing the give-and-take of the spectacle.

The following section will focus on three different elements of "looking" as explored in four films, all made by Italian directors within a ten-year span: 1) "Distance" in Pier Paolo Pasolini's *Salò, or The 120 Days of Sodom* (1975); 2) "Memory" in Dario

43

Argento's *The Bird with the Crystal Plumage* (1970) and *Deep Red* (1975); and 3) "Imagination" in Michelangelo Antonioni's *Blowup* (1966).

## "Distance"

Pasolini's final film, *Salò, or The 120 Days of Sodom*, is perhaps one of the most difficult and misunderstood films ever to be screened, and, arguably, depending on what you're inclined to believe, the primary cause for Pasolini's violent murder, which took place only a few weeks after he'd completed it. Loosely based on Marquis de Sade's writings, Pasolini chose to set his version of *The 120 Days of Sodom* in fascist Italy toward the end of World War II. The film, which is structured in four sections, each based on a circle of Dante's descent into hell, chronicles the abduction, degradation, torture, and murder of a group of young men and women at the hands of four predatory authority figures: the Duke, the Bishop, the Magistrate, and the President. The film takes place in an isolated, palatial Italian villa, the very splendor of which renders the violence committed within its walls as unthinkable.

According to writer Neil Bartlett, the film's four primary Fascist leaders "embody the four temporal and spiritual powers that brought into being the Italian Fascist dictatorship of 1944 and 1945—and that continued to participate through the 1970s in Italy's collective amnesia about its bloody, extremist past."[51] This "collective amnesia," as Bartlett refers to it, is similar to our idea of looking to the past as a method of lifting the veil. By showing an unwatchable representation of his country's past, Pasolini was tearing down the "self-protective and nourishing fantasy" afforded by the passage of time. Bartlett goes on to say that *Salò* "exists to give form to precisely that which is beyond imagining, to stage things that 'didn't' or 'shouldn't' happen. Its action is a series of obscenities and atrocities that most people would describe as 'unimaginable'; yet, with all the forces of a great imagination at its disposal, it makes you believe you are seeing them."[52] Of course, this echoes the impossibility of thinking the unthinkable, yet seeing it all the same, a concept inherent to our idea of the spectacle, which Pasolini exploits rather heavily in the film's final ten minutes. Referring to those final ten minutes, Bartlett writes, "Never has the mere act of watching felt so like victimhood, so like complicity, so like power—the unholy trinity of Fascist ideology that the film both embodies and dissects."[53]

*Salò*'s final sequence—most central to Bartlett's ideas—shows the four Fascist leaders as they take turns sitting in a chair before a window that looks out over the villa's courtyard. Using a pair of binoculars, each man watches the others torture and kill the prisoners with particularly horrific methods: eyeball gouging, burning and branding, genital mutilation, raping, scalping, hanging. The first to take his turn as a watcher is the Duke, whose point of view is shown magnified through the use of the binoculars. The choice Pasolini made to force viewers to see these atrocities in such a way is a prime example of what Bartlett referred to as the "complicity" of watching. By watching, we, as viewers, are both being victimized by the film (we are being shown something we do not want to see) and given power (we know, through our distance, that what we are watching is reprehensible). After watching the scene in the courtyard for a few minutes, and perhaps out of nothing more than curiosity, the Duke then turns the binoculars over in his hands and views the violence through an inversion of their display. He is literally distancing himself—and subsequently us as viewers—from the unthinkable. The implication here is that the viewer, in this case it is us ourselves, seeking to be entertained or enlightened by a film, must watch from a safe distance—and when things get too close for comfort, there is always falling back on that distance for feelings of self-protective and nourishing fantasy.

As Maurice Blanchot wrote: "Of whoever is fascinated it can be said that he doesn't perceive any real object, any real figure, for

45

what he sees does not belong to the world of reality, but to the indeterminate milieu of fascination.... Distance here is the limitless depth behind the image, a lifeless profundity, unmanipulable, absolutely present although not given, where objects sink away when they depart from their sense, when they collapse into the image."[54]

### "Memory"

A key element in many horror films is the guilt of the witness, or stories that revolve around somebody seeing something horrific happen and then being haunted by what they saw. Dario Argento is perhaps most well-known for his *giallos*—a sub-genre of horror he helped pioneer that incorporates elements of crime and mystery—in which the guilt of the witness is often employed as a plot device. His two most well-constructed and memorable *giallos* are *The Bird with the Crystal Plumage* and *Deep Red*. As a filmmaker, Argento is above all else a stylist, and *The Bird with the Crystal Plumage*, his debut as both writer and director, introduced many of the brilliant flourishes he would go on to popularize in his subsequent films. These hallmarks usually consist of childlike melodies on the soundtrack; meticulously rehearsed and arranged close-ups of murder utensils, black-gloved hands and photographic equipment; point-of-view shots from the killer's perspective; highly creative, sweeping camera movements; and glorified murder scenes.

*The Bird with the Crystal Plumage* tells the story of Sam Dalmas, an American writer living in Rome. One night, as he's walking home, Sam sees a violent scene on the mezzanine of an art gallery. Although the gallery is brightly lit and clearly visible through a floor-to-ceiling vitrine, Sam can only make out the legs of what appears to be two figures struggling with one another. By the time he crosses the street—narrowly avoiding being hit by a passing car—and reaches the outside of the vitrine, one of the two figures (dressed in all black) has jumped from the mezzanine and disappeared behind a door hidden in the wall, while the other (a red-headed women dressed in white) appears to have been stabbed. Sam enters the vitrine through an open, sliding-glass door and struggles with yet another sliding-glass door, this one leading into the gallery. There's a quick cut to a shot of a black-gloved hand pressing a red button, and then we see the door behind Sam close, effectively trapping him inside the massive display case—a housefly in a two-paned window. Helpless to intervene, Sam is now forced to watch the red-headed woman in the gallery suffer and plead for help. It isn't until a passerby notices that Sam is trapped that he is able to relay a message to call the police.

The red-headed woman lives through her attack, but something doesn't sit well with what Sam has seen. "There was something wrong with that scene," he tells the investigating detective, "something odd. I can't pin it down but I have a definite feeling that something didn't fit." Throughout the rest of the film, Sam is haunted by visions of the crime, reenacting the scene over and over again in his memory. To make matters worse, while he struggles to unravel a series of clues, hoping to get to the bottom of his obsession, several attempts are made on his life. "I feel that I'm getting close to the truth every minute," Sam says in the middle of the film. "The murderer is obviously of the same opinion—that's why he's trying to kill me. The more he tries, the more he risks discovery." The reason *The Bird with the Crystal Plumage* is such an interesting film, apart from its stunning quality of production, is because it's as much about solving a mystery as it is about the unreliability of memory—and the guilt that goes along with knowing that you've seen *something wrong*, something you were helpless to stop, something that you can't explain.

Blanchot: "Memory is freedom of the past. But what has no present will not accept the present of a memory either. Memory says of the event: it once was and now it will never be again."[55]

For the witnesses-cum-protagonists of Argento's films, viewing something horrific is often made worse by the tricks memory can play. This is an idea central to Argento's finest work in the *giallo* genre, *Deep Red*, a film which took many of the ideas central to *The Bird with the Crystal Plumage* and further refined them to the point of perfection.

*Deep Red* focuses on Marcus Daly, a pianist and music teacher at the conservatory in Turin. Much like Sam Dalmas in *The Bird with the Crystal Plumage*, Marcus is a character whose life is put in jeopardy after he sees something he shouldn't have—something he is helpless to put a stop to. Alone, making his way down a back alley near a large city square, Marcus happens to look up and see a woman with her palms spread against the glass of an apartment window, her mouth open, crying for help. A figure clad entirely in black appears behind her, bringing down a hatchet into her back. She falls forward, breaking the window. Marcus takes off running, entering the building, climbing the stairs, and making his way into the apartment. He moves cautiously down a long hallway, following the trail of blood. In his rush to find the injured woman, Marcus fails to notice that the hallway's walls are covered in strange, horrific portraits and disturbing artwork. One portrait, in particular, seems to take his attention, but not for long. A few, tense moments later and he's at the woman's side, lifting her corpse off the jagged shards of glass left in the shattered window's frame. Although it's far from obvious upon an initial viewing, Argento has already shown us the killer in the brilliantly edited and designed hallway sequence. This is what makes *Deep Red* transcend other, similar *giallos*. It is a movie that withholds nothing from its audience and its protagonist alike, effectively placing both in the same position of having seen something significant but not knowing what or why.

As the film progresses—much like Sam in *The Bird with the Crystal Plumage*—Marcus is continually haunted by the betrayal of his memory. "It's very strange," he tells a friend after the murder, "I don't even know if it's true or not, but when I went into that woman's apartment, the first time, I thought I saw a painting. But then a few minutes later it was gone." The plot of *Deep Red* becomes increasingly complex as Marcus investigates the image of that painting as he remembers it, eventually coming to believe that the painting represented something important, something that could trigger his memory. "That painting was definitely there," he says. "I didn't invent that. And so now, it's become a kind of a challenge—to my memory." Obsession leads Marcus to eventually overcome this challenge. And as he comes to realize what he's seen, we too, as viewers, come to realize that we have also seen it—whether or not we remember.

### "Imagination"

Both men in the *giallos* described above are obsessed with the idea that they are missing some key element of truth from what they have seen. Michelangelo Antonioni's *Blowup*, however, is about seeing something that appears to be the truth—and realizing that, upon closer inspection, all truth dissolves into nothingness. Antonioni's film is a thriller where nothing really happens. It's a film with no tension and no payoff. Instead, it asks viewers to consider the reality inherent to image—in this case an enlarged photograph—and the idea that it is our imagination that projects truths, half-truths and outright lies onto that which we see.

Taking place during the frenzy of London's 1960s fashion scene, *Blowup* creates a time and a place where outward beauty and trendiness mask a soulless world of polished surface, endless boredom, and cynicism. After growing disaffected with a stilted photo shoot, fashion photographer Thomas takes a walk through London's Maryon Park and becomes somewhat interested in a man and a woman who are either in a fight or enjoying a romantic tryst. Either way, their strangely passionate behaviors are interesting to Thomas, so he does what he does best: he turns the lens of his camera on them, watches closely, and fills up a roll of film with snapshots. He's far from subtle about his voyeurism and is soon confronted by the woman he has just photographed. She demands the film in Thomas's camera but he refuses to turn it over. Thomas then leaves the park and returns to his studio only to learn that the woman has followed him there.

To get rid of her, Thomas gives the woman a decoy roll of film. When she's gone, Thomas blows up the photos he took in the park and, in one of the images, discovers what he thinks may be a body. He continues blowing up the images, and as the prints become larger, the images they contain become blurrier. By attempting to get closer, to see more clearly, Thomas is in fact distancing himself from whatever truth he seeks. Antonioni's camera charts the sequence of images: a medium-distance shot of the woman dragging the man along by the hand, a fence running alongside the tree line behind them; the man's back facing the camera, his arms around the woman; a close-up of the man resting his head on the woman's shoulder in an embrace as she looks off into the distance, or perhaps, based on the spatial relations established by previous photographs, into the tree line; another medium shot of their embrace, only now there appears to be an unrecognizable blur behind the fence; a close-up of the blur that's difficult to make out but might depict a pair of eyes behind the branches; an extreme close-up of the barrel of a gun held in a man's hand; the woman, still held in the arms of the man, looking directly into Thomas's camera; now standing several feet apart from one another, the woman and the man both seem to realize that they are being watched; the man looking into Thomas's camera; an extreme close-up of the woman's face, betraying concern; the woman running toward Thomas with her hand before her face; a long-distance shot of the park, empty; a medium-distance shot of the woman with her back turned to the camera, standing over an unidentifiable blur on the ground; yet another medium-distance shot of the empty park.

Thomas returns to the park later that night and discovers the man's dead body, only he doesn't have his camera and so cannot capture any proof of this discovery. A noise in the dark scares Thomas off. The next morning, he once again returns to the park—only to find that the body has disappeared. Was it ever really there? It's possible that someone took it away during the night, but these sorts of hypotheticals are unimportant to Antonioni. This isn't a movie about tracking down a dangerous killer or exposing a shadowy conspiracy. Rather, *Blowup* is simply about the mystery of the image itself—the guilt it can instill in the viewer. In Thomas's case, the image briefly shows him a truth he is later unable to correlate with his reality. He cannot engage with any direct experience of things. Because of this, much like any truth he may have been seeking, Thomas disappears.

Salomon: "The role of witness enacts the central paradox of horror narrative. Something drastic happens—to the witness, to someone he or she observes. Yet what is witnessed has finally no firm basis in empirical causality and rather invokes some dimension of supernature, a dimension that suggests not so much the traditional supernatural as some chaotic element deconstructive of all conventions of ordering."[56] Within the concept of the spectacle, this chaotic element is any combination of distance, memory, and imagination—the three elements of viewership likely to deconstruct all conventions of ordering.

2.4: Giving In

Schopenhauer writes "What we fear in death is not in any way pain: for one thing, the latter obviously lies on this side of death; for another, we often flee pain into death just as well as, conversely, sometimes taking on the most horrific pain so as only, even when it would be quick and easy, to escape death for a little while longer."[57] Pain is a reminder that we are very much alive; it is body consciousness in its most urgent form. If one wills something if one lacks it and wants it, then death can certainly be willed by someone in terrible pain—as an escape. This, then, is what is meant by Nietzsche's "primeval reality": existence stripped of all comfort, wherein pain causes action as a means of survival. Until we are dead, there is no escaping the inevitable worst to come. And even then, there is no guarantee of relief. Blanchot: "if men in general do not think of death, if they avoid confronting it, it is doubtless in order to flee death and hide from it, but that this escape is possible only because death itself is perpetual flight before death, and because it is the deep of dissimulation. Thus to hide from it is in a certain way to hide in it."[58]

In this chapter, we have established that humans possess an insatiable need to view the suffering of others; that we often turn to artifice, or Apollonian art, to temporarily relieve this need; that our need to look while going beyond mere looking is explained by the idea of "lifting the veil," or seeking to relieve the horror within; and that viewership, or bearing witness, results in the internalization of guilt and is composed of three basic elements: distance, memory, and imagination. All of these ideas, when considered together, lead into the final aspect of the concept of the spectacle: *giving in*. Schopenhauer's idea that "we often flee pain into death" is particularly useful here in the sense that death can be considered relief from suffering inasmuch as it is the eradication of self. When faced with incomprehensible horror, we must relinquish the very thing that defines us as human: control—control of mind, control of body. Loss of control is an embrace of death in an attempt to flee pain in order to become something other than human. Again, Blanchot: "Why death? Because death is the extreme. He who includes death among all that is in his control controls himself extremely. He is linked to the whole of his capability; he is power through and through."[59]

If we define death only as becoming something other than human, then death can also be small pockets of "escape" from self. These moments of escape should be considered blank spots—or holes—in the fluid connection of body and mind. These holes can cause a temporary loss of control over the body, a literal forgetting of body consciousness, and, in turn, this loss of control can create a state of non-self not far removed from the nothingness of death. Moving forward, we will refer to this state of suspended being—the non-self being—as *the void*, which we will define as the decapitation of the mind from the body and the relief from pain found beyond the veil of the horror reality.

In an article written as a response to various writers and philosophers on the subjects of beheading and cinema, author Gary J. Shipley writes, "cinema's completion coincides with the decapitation of its captive audience. . . . The world does not stop at the eye or the head on its way in, or the self at those points on the way out. . . . And a universe anthropomorphically shrunk so as to fit inside a skull is wont to explode when that containing humanization is removed."[60] This idea of the cinema decapitating its captive audience echoes Bergson's concept of "pure memory," which is defined, loosely, as nascent perception, or perception that creates a response in the mind seemingly without the body's comprehension. Bergson: "My actual sensations occupy definite portions of the surface of my body; pure memory, on the other hand, interests no part of my body. No doubt, it will beget sensations as it materializes, but at that very moment it will cease to be a memory and pass into the state of a present thing, something actually lived."[61] For Shipley, the reality created by the images and signs of cinema is the reality of "a universe anthropomorphically shrunk" to fit neatly within the viewer's skull, perhaps displacing, however temporarily, the viewer's own memory and imagination (the self) with something wholly new. This newness is not correlated by the reality of the body in any way, besides the physiological act of the eye reacting to the light either projected by or onto the surface of the viewing screen, or the mind's calculations of distance between that screen and the body of which it is immediately aware. This cycle of the image filling the skull of the viewer and eradicating the self is what Shipley refers to as "the completion of cinema." We know that the human eye can perceive up to twelve images per second. Together, the movement-image and the time-image form an impression of reality not unlike that created by the relationship between the eye and the brain. Who's to say that life itself isn't actually a series of still images assembled by the brain as movement and time? Certainly we have no choice but to accept that what we see—and how we see it—is the truth. We must *give into* the new realities of the universes that cram the interior of our skulls.

And so we attempt, again and again, to flee reality by escaping into the void. This idea of escape through death is a trope that horror knows all too well. When the dark farmhouse is surrounded by the living dead and the rosy-fingered dawn seems like nothing more than a memory, there will always be someone who chooses to leave the terror of grappling with the inevitable worst-to-come behind, who chooses to flee into the waiting throngs of certainty—death itself. At the end of Pasolini's *Salò*, as the Duke, the Bishop, the Magistrate and the President commence their crowning atrocities, one of the prostitutes they've brought along to tell them stories, plays the piano in the parlor. When the torturing begins, the woman ceases her playing, walks to the nearest window, and jumps to her death below. In the film *Martyrs*, which we will discuss at further length in the final section of this book, a young woman who has been tortured by a secret organization intent on understanding the revelations gifted to those who pass over from one side to the other, whispers her secrets into the ear of a woman known only as Mademoiselle. In the next scene, Mademoiselle puts a gun into her mouth and pulls the trigger. Her last words to a colleague are that he should "keep doubting." Doubting that there may be anything other than nothingness beyond this life? Like the prostitute whose piano playing seems suddenly absurd in that terrible palatial villa, Mademoiselle is giving in as a means of ending the pain. And we cannot help but look and wonder and even doubt—after all it is what makes us human.

# Part Three: The Void

> *Holes*, she thought, and imagined how that must have been: going through life with gaps springing up, things that read as blank and empty spaces, as if the world were unfinished.
>
> –Brian Evenson

3.1: The Void (Within)

In her essay on abjection, *Powers of Horror*, Julia Kristeva defines *the void* as "the unthinkable of metaphysics."[62] This is a definition we will adopt as we continue to seek an understanding of the horror reality and its various components. If the horror reality is partly defined by our limited comprehension of the universe and an inability to communicate the strangeness of the world-without-us, and that, through looking, we have no choice but to accept that what we see—and how we see it—is the truth, then the unthinkable of our metaphysical understanding—seeking to answer the questions of *what is there* and *what is it like*—as referred to by Kristeva, will have to be further explored and, as much as possible, defined.

To begin, the void must not be the unthinkable thinkable (i.e., the center of the earth), which, by correlating with the natural order of things, cannot be considered *truly unthinkable*. The unthinkable can only be *that which lies beyond* comprehension. As such, the void can only be understood by lifting the veil and consequently being unable to correlate what we see with a previously understood or imagined reality. It is only when the natural order of things is truly unthinkable, when it becomes *un*natural, that the void will open as a sort of hollowing maw. The question then is where this opening occurs and, subsequently, how we can approach a comprehension of its opening. Because the mind is able to process sensations and understand abstract concepts that the body cannot, the void must then exist *within*. Consider it something of a cosmic infection: the unthinkable beyond (the outer) manifesting itself as a hole within (the inner) that serves to degenerate the whole—a corrupting blackness occluded by or swallowed within further blackness. It is here, within our own thoughts, that we flee pain into death. It is here, within our clumsy articulation of our feelings, where we attempt to build communication in order to share with others our understanding of existence, where we attempt to answer what is there and what it is like. Of course, we know we will always fail—whether due to inarticulate lucidity or articulate confusion. Because this failure is inevitable and self-fulfilling, another way to look at the void is as a whirlpool at the very core of being. Like Poe's descent into the maelstrom, it is a whirlpool whose existence cannot be relayed to any believing audience; the whirlpool simultaneously makes itself known as a disruption as it pulls comprehension of itself into a sort of hidden vacuum.

In order to fully understand this idea of holes within that degenerate the whole, we should turn to Reza Negarestani, who in his book *Cyclonopedia*—specifically in the chapter titled "Machines are Digging"—writes extensively on the so-called "( )hole complex." Defining the term, Negarestani writes that ( )hole complex "speeds up and triggers a particular subversion in solid bodies such as the earth. It unfolds holes as ambiguous entities—oscillating between surface and depth—within solid matrices, fundamentally corrupting the latter's consolidation and wholeness through perforations and terminal porosities."[63] If lifting the veil means being confronted with impossible images—sights glimpsed from beyond—then the result will be the internalization of the truly unthinkable. This inability to correlate what has been seen with the unthinkable thinkable can be considered a perforation in the fabric of reality. Too many perforations will inevitably lead to a porous being (create too many holes in the table beneath the black cloth and it will eventually fall apart). Negarestani refers to this process as a kind of "hollowing out," where the whole degenerates into a hollow body. This hollow body is the void manifesting its reality as the whirlpool at the core of being. Relating this idea to horror narrative, Negarestani turns to Lovecraft's concepts of cosmic menace from beyond time and space, saying that Lovecraft "addresses holey space or ( )hole complex . . . as the zone through which the Outside gradually but persistently emerges, creeps in (or out?) from the Inside."[64] We have already discussed how the outer can infect the inner, and will expand on the idea of horror as miasma (i.e., the inner infecting the outer) later in this chapter. Continuing, Negarestani writes: "Solid needs void to engineer its composition; even the most despotic and survivalist solids are compositional solids, infected by the void. Through these inter-collisions of void and solid, the Old Ones—according to Lovecraft—can revive their 'Holocaust of Freedom' (*The Call of Cthulhu*), both by consuming solid and by pushing compositions towards the highest degrees of convolution (as a result of the ambiguity of solid and void i.e. the fuzzy space of the hole and its surface dynamics."[65] According to Lovecraft's Cthulhu Mythos, the Old Ones were primordial beings, often entombed or hidden away beneath the planet's surface. They were city builders, architects of extradimensionality. Their ancient societies, now only partially understood through the ruins and artifacts left behind, are said to contain the secret knowledge of the beyond, but are buried within the very planet we call home. In that sense, in Lovecraft's universe, the earth itself is cosmically infected with the beyond.

This is the horror of the void: humans coming face to face with displacement, alienation, and the meaninglessness of life in the universe, seeking nothingness outside the self in an attempt at painlessness. In Lovecraft's fiction, the lucky ones are driven mad; the not-so-lucky are forced to continue living with whatever they have learned. The great revelations contained within Lovecraft's stories suggest that man's place among the stars lies in darkness. As Graham Harman writes, "Humans cease to be master in their own house. Science and letters no longer guide us toward benevolent enlightenment, but may force us to confront 'notions of the cosmos, and of [our] own place in the seething vortex of time, whose merest mention is paralyzing,' and 'impose monstrous and unguessable horrors upon certain venturous [humans]'"[66] (quotes within are taken from Lovecraft's "The Shadow Out of Time"). In this sense, the true purpose of the void is to create a portal to the beyond—from *within*. Much like the remnants of an ancient society created by primordial beings buried deep below the earth's crust, the void cosmically infects the inner with the outer. Essentially, the internalization of horror ultimately leads to a cosmic understanding of one's own meaninglessness.

The next question that concerns us is what must be done with this new knowledge. With this question in mind, we will return to the previously mentioned first paragraph of Lovecraft's "The Call of Cthulhu," this time excerpting the single sentence that concerns the concept of the void: "The sciences, each straining in its own direction, have hitherto harmed us little; but some day the piecing together of dissociated knowledge will open up such terrifying vistas of reality, and of our frightful position therein . . ."[67] The role of horror fiction can be seen as an attempt to piece together "dissociated knowledge" so as to open up "such terrifying vistas of reality." These vistas are what Meillassoux would refer to as "a world without thought—a world without the givenness of the world."[68] Such vistas can only exist as the void within. Previously, we demonstrated how the strangeness of the horror reality is created by cross-contaminated language. That language is often harnessed and arranged as narrative. What horror narrative does, then, is lift the veil for others who are perhaps unwilling or reluctant to do so. In this sense, horror has a miasmic effect. Above all other forms of narrative, horror can convey the void within by creating images of that which lies beyond—something approaching a cosmic understanding. This is how the inner can be released to infect the outer. One of the major difficulties faced by the writer of horror narratives, the creator of horror images, is how to provide a recognized context for this strangeness, or how to explain impossible things in a way that doesn't read as the ravings of a madman, or often worse, inane gibberish. Hence the preponderance of horror narratives told either as timeless tale passed down through generations or first-person testimonials of someone who has *seen* beyond. In most cases, these accounts will never truly be able to explain what terrible truths have been revealed, despite the fact that the teller has lived to tell about it.

This brings us to John Carpenter's film *In the Mouth of Madness*, a movie whose back cover copy reads, "this shocking story is, in the words of its acclaimed director, 'horror beyond description!'" This is a tall order for a horror narrative told primarily through dialogue and images. And yet it's my opinion that the film succeeds where so many other fail—it actually *does* create a sense of horror beyond description.

Bestselling horror author Sutter Cane writes Lovecraftian tales of terror that have, as his editor says, "an effect on his less-stable readers." That effect, an understatement if there ever was one, is that Cane's work literally turns his readers into homicidal maniacs. Just before the release of Cane's biggest and most anticipated book—which just so happens to bear the title of Carpenter's film—he disappears without a trace. Enter private investigator John Trent, a man particularly adept at sniffing out fraud. Trent is hired by Cane's publisher to track him down. He's paired with the aforementioned editor, a woman named Linda Styles. "For about a year before he disappeared," Styles says, "his work became erratic, bent, more bizarre than usual. He became convinced his writing was real, not fiction." In order to wrap his head around what he's dealing with, Trent reads Cane's fiction—

and begins suffering hallucinations. After some rather creative deductions, Trent and Styles follow the trail into Cane's fictional world, eventually crossing over into the small town of Hobb's End, despite its not existing on any maps. It's here that Trent and Styles learn the premise of Cane's new book: "It's about the end—to everything," Styles says. "And it starts here in this place with an evil that returns and takes over..."

Ironically enough, Trent's first conversation with Cane takes place through the screen of a confessional. Cane suggests that Trent read his new book. "The others have had a quite an effect," Cane says, "but this one will drive you absolutely mad. It'll make the world ready for the change. It takes its power from new readers and new believers. That's the point. Belief! When people begin to lose their ability to know the difference between fantasy and reality the old ones can begin their journey back." In the next scene, Cane hands over the newly finished, type-written copy of *In the Mouth of Madness* with orders to bring it back to the real world. With Styles affected by Cane's writing, Trent flees alone back into "reality" through a newly opened passage, hounded by Cane's monsters (we will return to this passage in the next section of this chapter). Back in the so-called real world, Trent's numerous and varied attempts to either discard or destroy the manuscript all fail; the book is either returned to him or reappears on its own. Finally, with seemingly no other options, Trent meets with Cane's publisher and warns that the publication of *In the Mouth of Madness* will effectively usher in the apocalypse—only to learn that not only has he already personally delivered the manuscript—months before—but that it has been in print for weeks. "I know this book will drive people crazy," Trent says. And the publisher responds, "Well, let's hope so. The movie comes out next month."

With the world descending into chaos, Trent wanders aimlessly into a movie theater and takes a seat, holding a bucket of popcorn. Carpenter's film ends with Trent's laughter as he watches the same film we have just watched, sees himself as he argues what is "reality" and what is "not reality." It's the only plausible ending to a horror film about "horror beyond description," or the miasma of the inner infecting the outer. It is a film about the transference of horror itself, the degeneration of what is only agreed-upon as "reality." And by seeking horror as entertainment, we too have been infected.

3.2: Puncture Wounds

Horror narratives are riddled with holes in both form and content: holes in the walls of once-safe places that let in evil, outside forces; holes made in the body that spill vital fluids.

In order to discuss how the void within is opened or accessed by these holes, we must differentiate between "form holes" and "content holes." For now, we will focus on "form holes"—or, as they are otherwise referred to by Negarestani, "plot holes." We will not be talking about inaccuracies in detail or chronology or the general sloppiness of writing that calls attention to its poor construction, but rather the so-called entry points (or exit wounds) through which horror narrative can be applied to our understanding of the world-for-us.

Much like the body becomes porous when the outer manifests itself as a hole within, so too does horror narrative degenerate, as a whole, when we apply its constructs to the world-for-us. Negarestani refers to this act as "Hidden Writing," which he defines as writing that "[utilizes] every plot hole, all problematics, every suspicious obscurity or repulsive wrongness as a new plot with a tentacled and autonomous mobility." He then goes on to clarify: "In Hidden Writing, a main plot is constructed to camouflage other plots (which can register themselves as plot holes) by overlapping them with the surface (superficially dynamic plot) or the grounded theme. In terms of such a writing, the main plot is the map or the concentration blueprint of plot holes (the outer plots). Every hole is a footprint left by at least one more plot, prowling underneath."[69] This kind of multilayered, porous quality allows horror narrative to function particularly well as metaphor or social commentary. The main plot can otherwise be considered the core idea of the story, perhaps even functioning as allegory, whereas the various "outer plots," or subplots, function to explore more specific instances of horror. Consider George Romero's genre-defining film *Night of the Living Dead*. The main plot of the film is concerned with the dead returning from the grave, hungry for human flesh. A small group of people take refuge in an abandoned farmhouse, under siege by hordes of the undead, and must learn to work together or face certain death. This plot, in the words of Negarestani, "is constructed to camouflage other plots." In *Night of the Living Dead*, these other plots, or "outer plots," could be considered any of the following: societal revolution; the collapse of militaristic/environmental experimentation; the justifications of euthanasia in the face of an unknown disease; and racial tensions in late-1960s America. These various outer plots are what Negarestani refers to as the "footprints" of the main plot. As such, these footprints are not always explicitly noticed upon initial readings or viewings of a horror story or film and are often taken in on a purely subliminal level (referring to the decapitation of the mind from the body, as discussed in the previous chapter). Subsequent readings/viewings often allow these footprints to come into focus—giving definition to what was previously "prowling underneath the main plot."

In a horror film like *Night of the Living Dead*, the core function of the main plot is to be applicable to the "world-for-us." As previously stated, this relegates the narrative to the realm of social metaphor or allegory. However, in order for the void to be present in horror narrative, the main plot must be applicable to the "world-without-us." The presence of the void allows for horror to exist beyond the natural order of things. The void cleanses horror of cheap thrills, the shallow frightfulness of the unthinkable thinkable, and propels fear into the cosmic realm of the unknown. This realm of the unknown—the void itself—is often reached by passages of some kind. Of course, passages usually connect two separate spaces, entranced by holes. It is these holes—and their consequent passages—that we will now refer to as "content holes."

There are three examples of content holes: 1) Holes that open up and either free something from a prison or let in something from beyond (portals); 2) holes that act as a transformative passage, warping whatever enters into a new and often unrecognizable form (transformers); and 3) holes in which the space within is endless and trapping (labyrinths).

## "Portals"

To continue our earlier writings on *In the Mouth of Madness*, we will now discuss the passage opened by Cane through which he sends John Trent from Hobb's End back into the so-called real world. After the scene with Trent and Cane in the confessional, within the depths of his church, Cane hands Trent the newly finished manuscript for his book and walks over to a rotting, reinforced wood door. "You take the manuscript back to the world for me," he says. "Go back. Your world lies beyond that passage." A sudden gust of wind blows through the room and Trent turns to see a long hallway that almost looks like something from one of Giger's paintings. Cane turns to the rotting wood door, which is swelling under pressure from whatever is on the other side. "Go now," he says, "I can't hold them back any longer." Then, providing one of the film's most memorable special effects, Cane raises his hand to his face and pulls away the image itself—as if it were nothing but paper. We see, on the underside of the rip in reality, the text from Cane's fiction, and beyond that, what Lovecraft would have referred to as "black seas of infinity." Trent walks to the newly formed rip and tentatively looks out into the darkness.

In a nice metafictional twist, Styles narrates the next scene while reading from Cane's hilariously exaggerated Lovecraftian prose: "Trent stood at the edge of the rip, stared into the illimitable gulf of the unknown, the Stygian world yawning blackly beyond. Trent's eyes refused to close. He did not shriek, but the hideous, unholy abominations shrieked for him, as in the same second he saw them spill and tumble upward out of an enormous carrion black pit choked with the gleaming white bones of countless unhallowed centuries. He began to back away from the rip as the army of unspeakable figures, twilit by the glow from the bottomless pit came pouring at him toward our world." Unable to convince Styles to come with him (she does, however, pass him the manuscript), Trent flees into the passage, pursued by the "unspeakable figures" of the gulf. I must mention here that this sequence, despite being fun in a cartoonish way, is one of the film's major failings. By attempting to portray abyssal horrors, Carpenter's special effects team instead gives audiences a parade of rubber monsters better suited to the schlocky b-movies popular in the 1940s and 50s. It's the one time that *In the Mouth of Madness* egregiously betrays its previously stated mission of portraying "horror beyond description." Though it is arguable that such a reference is intended, considering that later, hiding out in a hotel, the camp-favorite film *Robot Monster* is playing on the television. Either way, it strikes the wrong cord for this viewer.

Relating these events back to our various classifications of content holes, Cane's passage is an excellent example of a portal. The unholy abominations literally chase Trent back to "our world," where his experiences in Hobb's End continue to haunt him.

## "Transformers"

Of course, not every hole has something lurking in the abyss of the other side—sometimes the passage itself is its own horror. This brings us to the second variation of content holes, transformers, of which Junji Ito's manga "The Enigma of Amigara Fault," is a particularly good example. In "Enigma," a fault opens up, revealing a sheer wall of stone. The stone is perforated by hundreds, if not thousands, of human-shaped holes, each leading to an individual tunnel. Early in the comic, we are shown a flashback of a young man who comes face to face with the hole he believes is made for him. "This hole was made for me!"[70] he screams, scrambling up the rock face to enter it. Despite being drawn to the hole, and ignoring the protests of witnesses, he appears terrified by his own actions. "I have to go in!" he yells. This flashback is told by a young man to a young woman, Yoshida, who is also struggling with being drawn to her hole. "My silhouette is saying 'Come in,'" Yoshida says. "It's staring at me!"[71] In an effort to protect Yoshida from becoming lost in the stone, the young man piles rubble in the entrance of her body-shaped hole. Later that night, they retire to their campsite where Yoshida admits her fear of being left alone. "There is nothing lonelier than that hole," the young man says. "Do you see? The reason you were scared of the hole is because you were lonely."[72]

During the night, the young man recalls a nightmare. "I had committed a terrible crime and was about to punished,"[73] he says. Illustrations show the young man shirtless, dressed in slave rags, with his hands cuffed behind his back. He is surrounded by dozens of others similarly bound and dressed. "When someone committed a crime of my magnitude," he says, "the people of the past would dig human-shaped holes. Along the cliff walls were hundreds of holes for criminals executed in the past."[74] Inside the hole, the stone forms against his body as if vacuum sealed. "I had no choice but to keep moving forward. The stone felt cold all around me. To my horror my neck felt thinner and tighter as I moved on, getting longer and longer. Stretching to the point it should have been torn off. I felt a tug on my neck. And with time . . . my entire body felt more and more pressure as I moved on! Soon not only was my neck stretched but so were my arms and legs . . ."[75] The pairing of the continuous forward march and the stretching of the stone eventually deforms the young man's body until he is unrecognizable. This image startles him awake. Looking around the tent, he discovers that Yoshida has fled their campsite. Searching for her, he learns that she has removed the rubble he stacked up inside her hole and can only assume that she has entered the stone. Abandoned and terrified, he questions whether or not Yoshida's hole is actually *his own*—and enters after her.

Months later, we see a crew of workmen who have found the opposite side of the rock wall. Instead of recognizably human-shaped holes, they find grotesque squiggle-shaped holes. After questioning whether or not these holes are connected to the holes on the other side, one of the workers shines a light into the darkness and reveals the unrecognizable form of, we can only assume, the young man, now hideously malformed. "There's something slowly coming this way!"[76] one of the workers yells—a common reaction to coming face to face with a monster.

"Enigma" is about the transformative nature of the passage itself, giving into fear, and the monstrousness of loneliness. There is a reason that we refer to time's forward direction as "the passage of time." In the very act of living, we are being transformed into something that will eventually render us unrecognizable to ourselves.

### "Labyrinths"

The third, and final, form of content holes are labyrinths. In Brian Evenson's short story "The Sladen Suit," the labyrinth appears in the form of a rubber tube. Sladen suits, especially heavy and cumbersome diving suits, are entered through these tubes, which tightly conform to the shape of the body. Once the diver is inside the suit, the tube is then folded over to create a seal. Known by the men who wore them as "clammy death," the suits were problematic, overly complicated, and most likely terrifying to enter. Like the enclosing stone of the fault in "Enigma," the weight of the rubber tube would have been a claustrophobic squeeze—and sheer terror for anyone with a fear of enclosed spaces.

Evenson's story begins with an unnamed narrator telling us that he is the third man to enter the suit. "Under the watchful eye of the others," Evenson writes, "I unfurled the long rubber entry tunnel situated athwart the umbilicus and insinuated myself into it, breathing the stale sweat of the pair who had gone there before me and who were, to a man, dead."[77] Details are scant, but our narrator gives us just enough information to let us know that the men are lost at sea, their instruments are down and someone has murdered the captain. Not knowing what else to do, the men decide to throw dice to see who will dispose of the captain's body. Two men—brothers Tore and Stig—leave with the body; only one returns. It appears to be Tore, only the man claims, in fact, to be Stig. "For a few hours, he did not speak, did nothing but shake. Then, finally, in a whisper, he told us the story. He told us about the storm, that it was worse than it had been before, and that we were, in his opinion, unlikely to survive it. He told for us the death of Tore. *Stig, you mean,* we said. *No,* he said, *I mean what I say.*"[78] Hours later, Stig hears a noise coming from a voice pipe in one of the ship's hallways. Despite no one remembering the pipe existing before this moment, Stig claims to hear a voice from the other end. He listens to whoever is speaking through the pipe, turns to another crewman, and says "We can't wait out the storm and we can't escape by going onto the deck. We need instead to creep our way out. We need to escape through the Sladen suit." When asked who told him that, Stig says "Tore, of course."[79]

The men find the suit in the captain's office and Stig is the first to enter its rubber umbilicus. After initially appearing to become disoriented in the darkness of the tube, Stig makes his way to the suit and activates the rebreather. Through the faceplate, Stig appears to be frightened. He awkwardly makes his way down a corridor before falling over. The suit collapses, empty. The men decide to send in another with directions to signal from the inside. They draw straws and send in a man named Asa—but not before tying a rope around his waist. Like Stig, Asa disappears, leaving behind a crumpled, empty suit. Removing the rope, they discover its severed end is wet with blood. Finally, it is our narrator's turn. He will be, as we were previously informed, the third to enter the Sladen suit. After some struggle, he does make his way inside, only to discover that he cannot manage to find his way out. Evenson's descriptions of being enclosed inside the rubber tube are terrifying—and perfectly capture the horror of the labyrinth: "How long I was lost in that tunnel, I am unable to say. Perhaps hours, perhaps days, perhaps only minutes. At a certain point—or at an uncertain point, rather, I felt like parts of me were breaking loose, that layers of myself were smearing off against the sides of the tunnel and that there would be no getting them back. I began, I think, to scream, but that too was horrible, for it was like screaming into a rubber glove, and it made me feel that I was using up my little oxygen all the faster."[80]

Although the narrator of "The Sladen Suit" does manage to cut his way out of the tube—wielding the same knife that had previously been used to murder the ship's captain, no less—he finds himself abandoned by his fellow crewmen. "It was, admittedly, a ship very much like my own, almost identical in every particular, and as I explored it after having recovered sufficiently, I kept expecting to discover my companions. But the ship, from stern to stern, was empty. Apart from myself and the Sladen suit."[81]

By having damaged the suit in order to escape its labyrinth, the story's narrator has also ensured that he will never be able to get off the ship. It's an exit in the wrong direction, or an entrance into a term we will refer to as "the basement of the basement."

3.3: The Basement of the Basement

Although the Greek word *katabasis* has several different definitions, it is perhaps most closely aligned with either a trip to the underworld or traveling from the interior of a country to its coastline. A trip to the underworld is representative of the outer infecting the inner, whereas traveling to the coast is representative of the inner infecting the outer. In this sense, it is a concept that can be easily applied to our definition of the void, as well as literature in general (Dante's *Inferno*, Book XI of *The Odyssey*, as well as Orpheus's descent to the underworld all immediately come to mind as classic examples).

The underworld is that which is below—the other side of the mirror. And what is the coast of a landmass if not the entrance to the sea? Whose gradual decline into the blackest crags leads to the very basement of the planet? The point I'm trying to make is that wherever we find ourselves, whatever plane of reality is readily visible and deemed the "truth," there always exists the potential for *katabasis*. Whether it be fleeing a threat, or perhaps entering into one, our reasons for searching the limits of the surface of things are always an act of escape. Even remaining static, doing nothing, remains an act of escape from the potential threats that lie beyond immediate comfort. "What was?" Schopenhauer writes. "What is?—The will of which life is the mirror, and that cognition free of will which gets a distinct glimpse of itself in that mirror."[82] Here, Schopenhauer is talking about whether or not the past, once sealed away by death, gains a new existence. The memories of those innumerable lives lost will always remain, like impressions of a dream. The present is always infected by the dream-reality of the past, the calculations of foresight made to perceive the future. Much like the very planet we call home is surrounded by the vast reaches of outer space, each moment of waking life is separated from future and past and what remains as the immediate present is nothing but an endless sequence of interchangeable entrances and exits. *The basement of the basement*, then, as previously stated, is an exit in the wrong direction. By digging deeper than is wise, pushing through that which resists, a person in search of an exit will instead find only an infinite sequence of entrances. Likewise, a person in search of an entrance will find only an infinite sequence of exits. This endless sequence is a sort of suspension of time and space found in the basement of the basement. After all, a dark room with no exit out of, or entrance into, would contain no correlation to the natural order of things—its reality eventually meshing entirely with the strange logic of dreams. In the rooms of wrong exits, the very lack of correlation to the natural order of things escapes into an irreality. Blanchot: "'When we look in front of us, we do not see what is behind. When we are here, it is on the condition that we renounce elsewhere. The limit retains us, contains us, thrusts us back toward what we are, turns us back toward ourselves, away from the other, makes of us averted beings."[83]

This brings us to Hans Henny Jahnn's unsettling novella *The Night of Lead*. Published three years after Jahnn's death in 1959, *The Night of Lead* is a work almost singularly obsessed with the overlap of death and sexuality, eroticism and decay—and serves as an excellent example of the concepts and ideas inherent to the basement of the basement.

The story begins with foreboding words spoken by a disembodied voice: "'I'm leaving you now. You must continue on your own. You must explore this town which you do not know.'"[84] Although we never learn who says this (a clue is arguably given at the very end of the story), we are immediately introduced to our protagonist, Matthieu, a man abandoned beneath "a black sky with no stars."[85] The town itself seems to be both there and not there: "The facades were lit up, and appeared a uniform colour in the light, some being simply coated in shadows or muddied with dirt. Up above, the buildings disappeared in the black of the boundless sky. And every door and window was black, as if they were holes in front of the void."[86] With no other idea of what he should do, Matthieu walks toward a single illuminated window far away. Of course, as soon as he reaches the illuminated window, it goes dark, leaving him once more stranded in the void. "And with the window, the street lights extinguished too; or rather they now merely glowed without producing any appreciable light. It was as if a pall of black smoke had descended."[87] Matthieu continues on and is eventually stopped by a deep-voiced porter who hands him an invitation to the private residence of a woman named Elvira. Desperately seeking information as to where he is, or where he should be going, Matthieu's questions are met only with increasingly obtuse answers. Finally, perhaps in an attempt to end Matthieu's ceaseless questioning, the porter says, "There is no turning back here—always just one direction."[88] As if to prove his point, the porter takes Matthieu by the arm and shows him the way to a house, which seems to appear out of nothing. The porter departs as Matthieu is greeted at the door by a "groom" who refers to himself as Donkey. "I shall be at your side," Donkey says, "so that you won't make a wrong move. Apart from that, there are no rules in this house. Everyone behaves as they wish."[89] Donkey then escorts Matthieur to Elvira's chamber. "He felt at once that he had gone the wrong way, or was only in an antechamber. He heard the voice but could see no one, although the room was easy to take in: rectangular, with only a few pieces of furniture. . . . Apart from the door through which he had entered, there did not seem to be another."[90]

Jahnn's description of Elvira's room here is the first of many instances of a room of wrong exits to appear in *The Night of Lead*.

Essentially, everything told in the story thus far serves to establish a feeling of hopelessness and abandonment, of being suspended in time and place. When Elvira finally does appear, emerging from behind a concealed door, she further reiterates these themes with her dialogue: "Forget for the present your journey, and where you have come from. Your memories are anyway false. You wish to give purpose to your plan and to arrange your past so that it becomes meaningful."[91] Described only as a young woman dressed in a green silk gown, Elvira abruptly disappears behind the room's concealed door, once again leaving Matthieu abandoned and alone. To really hammer home this sense of isolation, Matthieu seems unable to even remember her appearance. "He stared at the hidden door, tried to reconstruct the image which had disappeared behind it. It remained incomplete . . ."[92] Donkey enters the room and informs Matthieu that Elvira is once again ready to see him. Now, the concealed door which had so recently served as an exit for Elvira, becomes an entrance for Matthieu. The interaction between Elvira and Matthieu quickly turns sour, and, in true dreamlike fashion, Elvira suddenly instructs Donkey to escort Matthieu away—with little reasoning behind her judgment. "We mustn't remain here," Donkey says. "We must carry on."[93]

Here begins the true journey of *The Night of Lead*. Matthieu and Donkey first leave behind Elvira's house, which is now given more descriptive detail than ever before—and yet even this description is filled with entrances-cum-exits, exits-cum-entrances. "They reached the door, entered a courtyard surrounded by a number of hushed buildings. A gateway led to a second courtyard, clearly similar to the first. And then a third courtyard."[94] Together, they leave the city and travel beyond its surrounding suburb. Donkey begins to grow cold and leans on Matthieu for support. They find an inn and enter, hoping to find warmth and food. Yet another bizarre scene ensues in which Matthieu realizes that Donkey is, in fact, a younger version of himself. "'We go to bed with our own self in the evening, but in the morning we see someone else in the mirror.'"[95] From this point forward, Donkey instructs Matthieu to refer to him as Other. After they attempt to order drinks and food—it turns out that the restaurant is completely out of stock of everything—Matthieu and his younger self must, once more, journey into the blackness of the night. Only now, as they discover upon leaving the restaurant, it is snowing. "The realization alarmed [Matthieu] greatly; he also felt a dust of snowflakes alight on his face and hands. He took a few steps on to the street; then without even asking Other, attempted to go back into the inn. The closed door no longer opened."[96] Yet again, Jahnn ushers his characters forward into the unknown with no hope of return. And to make matters worse, whereas earlier Donkey was cold, Other is now beginning to freeze. Other suggests they return to his home, which he refers to as "the cellar." "'My home,'" he says, "'it is terrible there. It is a place to die in. I did not want to die, but now I realize that I will just as certainly expire out here.'"[97] With no other option, Matthieu resorts to carrying Other through the snowstorm. "He had been commanded to carry a person through the snow, to carry on until he reached a goal he did not know—or a stop became necessary—until it proved impossible to carry on."[98]

The two men do, eventually, reach Other's home, which is essentially nothing more than a door in a wall that leads to a long, steep flight of stairs. Lighting matches to guide their way, they descend into a cellar. "The stairs were long, straight, enclosed by walls. As the feeble light of the flame died, they groped their way down in the darkness."[99] From here, the stairs descend even deeper before arriving at yet another door. "But the door did not open easily. The youth used another match, and Matthieu saw that there was no lock in which to insert a key. It consisted of a couple wooden boards which were distributed over a number of roughly hewn uprights, which Other pushed inwards in a particular order. As he moved the last door swung open. Blackness returned at once, and in blackness the two of them crossed the threshold."[100] This scene in *The Night of Lead* literalizes the term *the basement of the basement*, as Other reveals that he sleeps in a hole in the ground, below "a trapdoor that could have led to the dusty coffins of a catacomb."[101] Other enters his bed in the floor and hints that he is dying. "'It is too late to turn back,'" he says. "'All the doors are closed. All the streets are blocked. You have recognized who I am. You know that you have met your own self. There can be no more refuge in lies.'"[102]

The final movement of *The Night of Lead* deals with the idea of self-eradication. It is revealed that Other is grievously injured and wishes to flee his pain into death. Matthieu is faced with the task of killing his younger self. "The young man's torment filled him with horror. Horror and a mysterious indecision."[103] And in the final pages—a bravura act of existential horror—Mattieu descends into the utter blackness from which he sprang. "Fear, until now constantly suppressed or thwarted by paltry hopes, had overwhelmed life. He surrendered to it with dull horror. He felt his brain sweat and this inner perspiration became a dissipating poison, an inner darkness corresponding to that surrounding him."[104]

Up until this point, Matthieu's descent into horror has been an articulate confusion. And yet with so much failure of language in *The Night of Lead*, it is only when Matthieu's "inner darkness" corresponds to "that surrounding him" that he is finally released from indecision and confusion. Matthieu has learned to embrace the horror reality. And by merging with existence in the present, by accepting being with no past and no future, suspended in the void, he has performed a true act of *katabasis*.

3.4: Horror Vacui

To quote once more from the opening paragraphs of Lovecraft's "Supernatural Horror in Literature," in which he is talking about the potential for horror to move beyond simple murder and ghosts that have long ceased to be frightening: "A certain atmosphere of breathless and unexplainable dread of outer, unknown forces must be present; and there must be a hint, expressed with a seriousness and portentousness becoming its subject, of that most terrible conception of the human brain—a malign or particular suspension or defeat of those fixed laws of Nature which are our only safeguard against the assaults of chaos and the daemons of unplumbed space."

It is this idea of the "dread of outer" that makes the opening of the void within horrific. If there were no dread, no suspense leading up to something entirely unknown, the opening of the void would just be something—like any other thing—that happens and is then forgotten. The dread is a direct byproduct of the realization that whatever passage opens up, whatever is waiting on the other side, might be more painful, more "malign" than the natural order of things in accepted reality, which Lovecraft here refers to as "those fixed laws of Nature" (we will further discuss the idea of the malign universe in the next chapter). There is little use fighting the porousness of being. Like the last man standing in the face of impossible odds, a man who has no choice but to give in, who flees pain into death so as to become something other than human, the opening of the void is the result of having no available exit other than succumbing to "unknown forces." This is "that most terrible conception of the human brain," that things are never quite what they seem—for reasons we will never quite understand.

As we have discussed previously, the insidiousness of the void within is its whirlpool-like hiddenness. Much like nature abhors a vacuum and will seek to immediately fill an empty space, the natural order of things, once punctured, will seek to immediately fill the void with "the assaults of chaos." Such a *horror vacui* is made literal in the "Stygian world yawning blackly beyond" in Carpenter's *In the Mouth of Madness*. The blackness beyond Cane's words unleashes horrors that literally chase John Trent back into an altered, haunted reality—a horror beyond description, indeed—a horror reality carved out in the unending shadows of the basement of the basement.

"It's funny, isn't it?" Cane says. "For years I thought I was making all this up. But they were telling me what to write." And what could be more horrific than this—the revelation of a controlling power behind all creation? To be a puppet on the end of a string?

This dread, tucked away tight within the deepest recesses of the void, is the engine powering our need to "create" new fictional realities. These stories, our images—they are what Lovecraft refers to as "the daemons of unplumbed space." Cane's words here, no doubt fed to him from beyond, are evidence of suspended being, an admission that crosses over the abyss separating motivation from possession.

And then there is Mark in Andrzej Zulawski's film *Possession*, whose wife Anna seems to miscarry a squid-like manifestation of anxiety and dread, perhaps caused by their disintegrating relationship, a manifestation that later evolves into a doppelgänger of Mark himself, eclipsing his life in its final moments. Speaking to her lover, Anna justifies her murderous protection of the creature she miscarried, "You are not different from anyone else. We are all the same, but in different worlds, different bodies, and different versions—like insects." This is the horror of being possessed by our greatest fears, those awful feelings of self-loathing, concentrated hatred of self, resentment of being. And what is possession if not the invasion of supposedly evil spirits, miscarrying an abomination, something uninvited that is animating the body in unwanted ways? In this sense, writing horror is something of an exorcism. And we exorcise these demons, these creatures we hide away and nourish, in an effort to possess or infect others—filling that vacuum in space—to essentially share with others that which fills us with dread. We cannot bear to stomach it alone, so we turn to the other. As Blanchot writes, "When I am alone, I am not alone, but, in this present, I am already returning to myself in the form of Someone. Someone is there, where I am alone."[105]

# Part Four: Black Seas of Infinity

> One has in all sorts of ways attempted to bring the immense greatness of the cosmos into closer proximity to everyone's power of comprehension, and then from there taken the occasion for edifying considerations, such as regarding the relative minuteness of the earth, not to mention of human beings; or to the contrary in turn, regarding the greatness of the spirit within this so minute human being, who is able to discover, grasp, even measure this cosmic magnitude . . .
>
> –Arthur Schopenhauer

> Passing through the memories of a thousand years, a fiction without scientific objective but attentive to religious imagination, it is within literature that I finally saw it carrying, with its horror, its full power into effect.
>
> –Julia Kristeva

4.1: The Dissolve

Thacker: "what genre horror does is . . . it takes aim at the presuppositions of philosophical inquiry—that the world is always the world-for-us—and makes of those blind spots its central concern, expressing them not in abstract concepts but in a whole bestiary of impossible life forms . . ."[106] The construction of narrative—Michelstaedter's rhetoric—with its easily understood and digestible language, its comforts, is being used to instill larger, more abstract ideas in the reader, or, in the case of horror narrative, exposing them to the miasma. A horror story in which the characters stand around and spook one another with grand philosophical statements wouldn't be much of a horror story at all. Indeed the most effective horror presents visions understood as terrifying if not only for their taking place in the world-for-us.

Therefore, in order to "think about the world-without-us philosophically," as Thacker has written, we must better understand what we have earlier referred to as correlationism. Although we touched on this idea in "Toward a Horror Reality," albeit briefly, when we stated that correlationism is "the idea that our existence is limited to the correlation of thinking and being," we must now expand on this definition in order to better understand its importance to the concept of horror beyond description.

Ray Brassier writes, "Correlationism is subtle: it never denies that our thoughts or utterances *aim at* or *intend* mind-independent or language-independent realities; it merely stipulates that this apparently independent dimension remains internally related to thought and language."[107] To summarize: the world-for-us is understood only in relation to ourselves. This idea has been dominant in metaphysics since the eighteenth century, when Kant gave voice to the so-called philosophy of finitude. Speculative realism, although still cohering as a philosophical tendency, has gone to great lengths to break free of this idea, to provide arguments that support Brassier's statement that "although thought needs being, being does not need thought."[108] Such thinking greatly helps us articulate the idea of horror beyond description. As we have previously stipulated, horror stories often explore the unknown, or what we have called *that which lies beyond*. Horror narrative, then, in order to be horrific and not abstract, must somehow relate that which lies beyond to the world-for-us. It must provide some sort of correlation for the reader—a bridge spanning the known and the unknown, the thinkable and the unthinkable, the possible and the impossible.

Again, Brassier, this time from his essay "Concepts and Objects":

> "To say that I can think of something existing independently of my thought need not be flagrantly contradictory once I distinguish the claim that my thoughts cannot exist independently of my mind, which is trivially true, from the claim that *what* my thoughts are about cannot exist independently of my mind, which simply does not follow from such a trivial truth. ... The fact that I cannot think of an uninhabited landscape without thinking of it does not mean that this landscape becomes inhabited merely by virtue of my thinking about it. ... The correlationist conceit is to suppose that formal conditions of 'experience' (however broadly construed) suffice to determine material conditions of reality. But that the latter cannot be uncovered independently of the former does not mean that they can be circumscribed by them."[109]

As Ligotti writes, "When someone says she has not been feeling her old self, our thoughts turn to psychology, not metaphysics. To reason or to hold as an article of faith that the self is an illusion may help us to step around the worst pitfalls of the ego, but the mitigation is light-years from liberation."[110] By emphasizing the distinction between "reason" and "faith," Ligotti further underlines the importance of the *strangeness*, or the embracing of the inherent contradictions of religious thinking (superstition) and scientific rigor (reason). The strangeness is the one constant in the horror reality: thought in need of being. "No thing in the world has cause for its existence plain and simple," Schopenhauer writes, "but only a cause by which it exists precisely here and precisely now."[111] Here then is what Lovecraft meant when he wrote of the black seas of infinity, upon which "it was not meant that we should voyage far."

In the previous three chapters, this book has presented the argument that the horror reality is partly defined by our limited comprehension of the universe and an inability to communicate the strangeness of the world-without-us, and that, through looking, we have no choice but to accept that what we see—and how we see it—is the truth. Attempting to relate this so-called truth to our own existence leads to the opening of the void within, which connects the world-for-us and the world-without-us. As such, the final element of this argument will be *the dissolve*, or the idea that horror can only exist as the end result of some sort of misfired correlation. The final horror, then, is that which takes us full circle to the inevitable failure of language—the eradication of self; to become something other than human. This is the inevitable worst to come—*the dissolve* of correlation into what we will refer to as *the speculative unknown*.

By embracing the idea that impossible life forms—anything from abyss-lurking squid-faced men to sentient planets to regular everyday objects—can exist without thought, speculative realism's refusal to accept philosophies of finitude as an endgame can help us to better understand our idea of the horror reality by offering a way of better understanding what we have referred to as horror beyond description.

4.2: Horror Beyond Description

By accepting our non-comprehension of the horror reality we are in fact affirming its existence. In other words, by acknowledging the existence of a horror beyond description, we are leaving the door open for speculation. And like Bergson's idea that an image might be present without being represented, speculation allows us to acknowledge that which goes beyond being immediately apparent—perhaps as a mechanism that functions in order to give our lives meaning. After all, if horror can be defined by Lovecraft's belief that "the oldest and strongest kind of fear is fear of the unknown," then we can take comfort in the fact that, however bleak or comfortless life may seem, it could always be worse.

Of course this notion of horror, of fear of the unknown, would not exist without consciousness of the self. With this in mind, the speculative realist aspects of the horror reality—or being without thought—must be differentiated from a more generalized notion of so-called metaphysical horror—or thought needing being. These two concepts, naturally, are antithetical to one another, as metaphysical horror occurs as a sort of incomprehension of the world-without-us, resulting in a reaffirmation of self (horror cannot exist without a witness). The horror reality, on the other hand, offers us a method of articulating being without thought (horror exists that cannot be witnessed). This is the core of what makes horror narrative such an effective means of communication. Here, the implied message goes something like "speculate all you like, but you'll never truly grasp the inevitable worst to come." Like Cane's admission that the transformative power of his words is not actually his own, the horror reality acknowledges that the world-for-us, or that which is meaningful, is as fundamental to our notions of self as the world-without-us, or that which cannot possibly be understood. This, once again, is the outer manifesting itself as a hole within the inner. Take comfort in meaning all you'd like; believe that your language connects you to others in meaningful ways—it will always be overshadowed by the horrific implications of speculation.

In the stories of cosmic-horror writer Laird Barron, even the smallest of otherwise innocuous actions—the opening of a doorway, the snick of a lighter in a darkened cave—can shift the universe off its axis. The realities created by Barron are never wholly isolated, existent unto themselves, but rather dependent on some *other*, some larger, malevolent intelligence harboring no need for humanity beyond a carnivorous desire for meat and bone. In this sense, Barron is not only building on Lovecraft's tradition of the indifferent, omnipresent universe, but also taking it one step further. What if the universe itself were not indifferent, but malign?

In Barron's story "Procession of the Black Sloth," the horror inherent to speculation becomes apparent when the very seams of reality pull apart from one another, exposing a reality that can only be described as horrific, a reality that is *lived in* rather than witnessed, whose scope and implications aren't understood by those confined within its abyss as much as they are experienced. This is a grand reveal in the tradition of the magician, that black wizard, who, upon waiting for maximum dramatic effect, pulls away the curtains of reality and offers a glimpse of the mind-bending. How discomfiting to discover that we, the audience, were the magician's subjects all along.

Dispatched to Hong Kong to work for technology manufacturer Coltech Ltd., Royce Hawthorne is tasked with posing as a quality assurance consultant in order to investigate what appears to be run-of-the-mill industrial sabotage. His first order of business is to weasel his way into the graces of Brendan Coyne, a communications consultant suspected of funneling secrets to Coltech's competitors. Royce spends his nights getting accustomed to his apartment complex, the Lord Raleigh Arms, or "the LRA" as it's referred to by its residents. The LRA appears pleasant enough on the surface, but a closer examination soon reveals hidden dimensions. "Friendly residents warned that despite evidence of extensive remodeling, such cosmetics masked a host of problems. Plumbing leaked and power came and went at inopportune moments. At such times, the elevators were out of service, and the air conditioning offline. Then, the residents of Lord Raleigh Arms endured the blackness of sweltering apartments and listened to cockroaches scrabble in the hollow spaces behind freshly painted gypsum."[112] This idea of surfaces being untrustworthy, of "cosmetics" masking "hollow spaces" beyond what's readily apparent is echoed again and again as Royce uncovers nothing as mundane as cutthroat profiteering, but rather an all-encompassing hell whose punishments seem uniquely designed to reflect his own guilty conscience.

By passing his nights at a local cocktail lounge frequented by industry players, Royce is able to become something of a confidante for Coyne. Astute and always asking the right questions, Royce learns that Coyne lives in a nearby building with his elderly mother, a woman whose closest friends weirdly seem to congregate in the quadrangle of complexes surrounding the LRA. Perhaps following a hunch, Royce spies on these women—chief among them one Agatha Ward. He even goes so far as to hire a teenager, Chu, to make surveillance tapes of their daily lives.

One night, over drinks at the lounge, Coyne reveals that Agatha is something of a spiritual leader for the other women, not excluding his mother. They appear to have some sort of society or organization established for themselves, he explains, which they obscurely refer to as the "Procession of the Black Sloth."

Meanwhile, the LRA is becoming increasingly terrifying; Royce's nights in his apartment are filled with noises and strange occurrences, odd happenings and nighttime visits. Royce receives a videotape through the mail that appears to have been sent from

Chu—particularly alarming considering the fact that Chu has been missing for weeks. Even more alarming is that the tape, rather than being the kind of surveillance tape Chu had previously supplied Royce with, actually turns out to be something of a skillfully produced documentary. Describing the tape's contents, Barron writes, "An old, old heavyset Chinese woman in a nurse's pinafore was giving the unseen narrator a tour of what seemed to be an abandoned sanitarium. She carried a flashlight and swept its watery beam over ceilings that leaked plaster and stringers of wiring. Piles of debris littered the corridor. The corridor was notched by small white iron doors. She stopped at each door, pointed and muttered into the camera." Barron continues, "When the camera zoomed in on her pointing finger, one could resolve metal placards with lettering. 2: CHAMBER OF GRINDING, said one. 8: CHAMBER OF MOUNTAIN OF KNIVES, said another. . . . She came to a larger door set into a slab of masonry. The door was barred and heavily corroded by rust. Its placard read: BLACK SLOTH HELL."[113] Upon initial reading of this scene, the reader is given to understand that Royce is witnessing these images as they are presented by the screen of his television. However, a closer read reveals that the images of the so-called BLACK SLOTH HELL create a puncture wound in Royce's reality, leaving him trapped in a labyrinth of illusions and wrong exits.

Our first inkling of this altered reality—this glimpse of the horror reality—arises when, after Royce is physically unable to witness anymore of these images, he awakes not in his apartment but in a totally different place. "Royce's skull felt like an anvil. He rose to make for the bathroom and almost tripped over a body. Before he could yell, the lights came up, revealing the bald furnishings of a decrepit theater. The projector was still shuttering, splashing arcane symbols on the screen. . . . He rushed to the lobby and accosted the girl sweeping popcorn from the carpet. She recoiled from his urgent demands for information. What theater was this? When had he arrived? Who'd brought him here?"[114] This is the intrusion of the malevolent universe. With this undoing of the natural order of things, Royce's reality collapses. He dissolves into a world whose laws seem governed wholly by the speculative unknown. As Barron later writes, detailing yet another one of these puncture wounds, "It came back to him then, how he'd been trying to find the news, but every channel was filled with either black static, or the repeating image of a chamber filled with dozens of screaming people." Increasingly, Royce's only option is to give in, or to flee reality by escaping into the void within. "He couldn't shake the stupor that descended upon him, that rendered him a helpless observer to his moving hands."[115] Like the doorways that lead only to wrong exits in *The Night of Lead*, and, much like Matthieu at the end of that story, Royce's inner darkness eventually corresponds to "that surrounding him." For example, in a particularly brilliant sentence, Barron writes, "[Royce] dug his fingers into the [door] frame, half-expecting the world to tilt and drop him into an abyss of starry sky."[116]

When Royce finally does come face to face with what we can only imagine is the malevolent force responsible for the horror reality, he is, as should be expected, unable to comprehend its very unknowability, instead correlating its surface appearance with a traumatic figure from his memory. As we previously mentioned, nothing in this story is quite what it seems, and the recognizable surfaces of things are merely slathered with gaudy cosmetics.

For these reasons, "Procession of the Black Sloth" provides an example of the extreme end of the horror reality, a glimpse into the black machinations of powers beyond our understanding, one of many truly excellent stories Barron has produced in his remarkable career. In this case, the revelations in "Black Sloth" go beyond the mere act of witnessing the horrific—the act of correlation—at the core of so many horror narratives, and venture bravely into the speculative unknown—the larger sense of searching that, inevitably, leads to a sense of almost cosmic paralysis, or pure dread. Barron's accomplishment here is something of a reverse cosmic infection, a cosmic return, in which the contaminated inside boils over, chemically altering the outside. By dissolving into the speculative unknown, Royce succeeds in eradicating any lingering sense of self, his inner darkness becoming indeterminate with that which surrounds him. And yet there is no relief to be found. Here, at the bottom of the abyss, that timeworn and comforting adage of "it could always be worse" no longer applies. One thing we can be sure of, however: what remains can only be speculated.

4.3: Speculative Annihilation

As we discussed earlier, the genre of horror has traditionally looked to the ghosts of the past for inspiration. In the twenty-first century, however, horror is beginning to change. Fundamental to this change is the increasingly apparent awareness of our limited comprehension of the universe and an inability to communicate the strangeness of the world-without-us. This breakdown, in turn, has led to the creation of what we can consider to be a new kind of narrative: the narrative of extinction. Blanchot: "Existence is authentic when it is capable of capable of enduring possibility right up to its extreme point, able to stride toward death as toward possibility par excellence. It is to this movement that the essence of man in Western history owes its having become action, value, future, labor and truth. The affirmation that in man all is possibility requires that death itself be possible: death itself, without which man would not be able to form the notion of an 'all' or to exist in view of a totality, must be what makes all—what makes totality—possible."[117]

Less concerned with the unalterable past—that which has brought us to the point of the present—the narrative of extinction sets its sights on the unknown—or that which lies ahead. In this sense, it has much in common with the horror reality, which is ultimately concerned with nothing less than our collective annihilation as a species—a fear compounded by its very inevitability. As Eugene Thacker writes, "In our era of natural disasters, climate change, global pandemics, and the ongoing specter of bioterror, we are continually invited to think about humanity and its relation to its real, hypothetical, or speculative extinction."[118] Traditionally, the narrative of horror has always functioned as a way of contemplating the aspects of reality that scare us. Now, reality has outdone even horror, and presented us with the truly unthinkable: the extinction of all life. The argument over being-without-thought has never been so readily apparent.

As Brassier writes in his book *Nihil Unbound*: "Extinction is real yet not empirical, since it is not of the order of experience. It is transcendental yet not ideal, since it coincides with the external objectification of thought unfolding at a specific historical juncture when both the resources of intelligibility and the lexicon of ideality are being renegotiated. In this regard, it is precisely the extinction of meaning that clears the way for the intelligibility of extinction. Senselessness and purposelessness are not merely privative; they represent a gain in intelligibility. The cancellation of sense, purpose, and possibility marks the point at which the 'horror' concomitant with the impossibility of either being or not-being becomes intelligible."[119]

How many years do we have left on this planet? 100? Maybe 200 if we're lucky? It seems that, with every passing decade, these speculations are becoming more specific—and the amount of years predicted is becoming fewer (a good example of this is Darh Jamail's 2013 article "The Coming 'Instant Planetary Emergency," published in *The Nation*, in which Jamail chronicles the ever-shrinking timeline of when climate change will eradicate all life on earth). We do know for certain that the global population will reach ten billion at some point during this century, that a global famine is imminent, that wars are more likely to be waged over bodies of fresh water rather than stockpiles of nuclear arms. But none of this is new—none of this is shocking. Such statements, despite their urgency, remain largely abstract for those living in the first world.

"Every species can smell its own extinction," says John Trent toward the end of *In the Mouth of Madness*. "The last ones left won't have a pretty time of it. And in ten years, maybe less, the human race will just be a bedtime story for their children. A myth. Nothing more." Trent's thinking here obviously implies that "something other" will survive our own extinction. But what if our extinction was total? Of this, Thacker writes "if absolute extinction implies that there can be no thought of extinction, then this thought in itself leaves but one avenue open: that extinction can only be thought, that it can only be said to exist, as a *speculative annihilation*."[120] And then, "The infamous question 'What is life?' appears to always be eclipsed by the question 'What is being?' And yet the very idea of Life-without-Being would seem to be an absurdity for philosophy . . . though as we've seen, not for horror."[121]

Or, to put it yet another way, we turn to the discomfiting words of Toshi Ryoko, the twisted behavioral ecologist in Laird Barron's story "The Forest," who says: "Evolution is a circle—we're sliding back to that endless sea of protoplasmic goop."[122]

Horror overcomes the impossible by providing answers, whether supernatural or rooted in the natural order of things, in response to speculation. Images of horror will always be interpreted as relating to the body. Here is the full power into effect of horror, or "a fiction without scientific objective but attentive to religious imagination" as Kristeva says—once again, the strangeness. What Kristeva is expressing here is a way of answering that question which has plagued mankind since the birth of consciousness: What is being? Horror allows us to philosophically engage with this question, to philosophically engage with life itself, while simultaneously correlating the absurdity of our responses with the natural order of things. In other words, in order to consider the existence of impossible life forms, we must reaffirm our own body consciousness. And by reaffirming our own body consciousness, we will reaffirm the existence of the world-without-us. Horror, then, is the permission to speculate beyond our own limitations as a species, including an inability to progress beyond base savagery, to overcome the inherent failure of communication, and to truly understand the concept of being without thought.

Here, we once again return to the film *Martyrs*. Earlier, we mentioned the character Mademoiselle, who becomes privy to the visions of a young woman who has seen beyond death. Access to these visions is granted, first, by creating a victim. As Mademoiselle explains, "You lock someone in a dark room. They begin to suffer. You feed that suffering, methodically, systematically and coldly. And make it last. Your subject goes through a number of states. After a while, their trauma, that small, easily opened crack makes them see things that don't exist." In this case, what can be seen are monsters—images manifested by trauma. Like Bataille and his *Story of the Eye*, trauma is at the root of the return of the past; it haunts the darkest corners of our memory. *Martyrs* goes beyond these images and looks into the unknown. This is accomplished, first, by differentiating between "victims" and the titular "martyrs." As Mademoiselle says, "People no longer envisage suffering . . . That's how the world is. There are nothing but victims left. Martyrs are very rare. A martyr is something else. Martyrs are extraordinary beings. They survive pain, they survive total deprivation. They bear all the sins of the earth. They give themselves up. They transcend themselves."

The extreme amounts of pain these martyrs are forced to endure results in a transfiguration. Through suffering, these victims are able to "see" beyond the immediate reality of mortality. Here, we have a group of people using rigorous methods to transcend beyond the flesh in an attempt to attain the divine. In other words, they are embracing the strangeness. As Mademoiselle says, "Don't try to tell me that the notion of martyrdom is an invention of the religious."

In the film, a young woman named Anna is systematically broken down as described by the methodology above. Eventually, her captors begin the "final stage" of her torture. They strap her into some sort of custom gyroscope where she is skinned. In what we can only imagine is unbearable pain, Anna is then suspended from an iron bar by her wrists in a manner similar to crucifixion. Describing her state, one of her captors says "She's let go, completely let go . . . I swear she no longer sees anything around her." Still alive, though perhaps only in the most technical sense, Anna's eyes remain open, angled upward—fixated on something that only she can see. In a sequence reminiscent of the interstellar tunnel of colored light toward the end of Kubrick's *2001: A Space Odyssey*, we discern a radiant halo of light in the black of Anna's pupil, as if suspended in a void. The light grows in intensity until it is all-encompassing. Although we can only speculate as to what that light might represent, what is certain is that these torture sessions were designed not only to allow the victim to see what lies beyond death—to be entirely at one with herself and the world, persuaded—but to live long enough to offer testimony, rhetoric. "Did you see?" Mademoiselle asks. "The other world?"

We already know that whatever testimony Anna is able to give inspires Mademoiselle to take her own life—but not before she tells her colleague to "keep doubting." Without doubt, there would be no need for speculation, as the immediately apparent reality would remain unquestioned. As we know, however, things are never quite what they seem. The world-for-us is filled with illusions. Like the end of the world as depicted in *In the Mouth of Madness*, and the inescapable, malign reality of "Procession of the Black Sloth," *Martyrs* can be interpreted as an exploration of a horror beyond description, a speculative annihilation of both the self and humankind as a whole. This is horror evolved.

4.4: The Spectacle of the Void

As long as we're alive, using our bodies to fill space and peer into the darkness, all of our problems—both individually and collectively—will return to a fundamental inability to communicate. All language is failure. When things break down, as they always do, we will struggle with even more intensity, thus quickening the deterioration.

Considering the central importance of language in our lives, what other choice do we have? It's difficult to argue that anything more significant, more destructive than language has ever been, or possibly could be, inflicted upon the human race. Everything beyond this realm is the void. Like Hecker in "Mudder Tongue," without the capability to produce and interpret language, we would be something other than human.

But what is an "other" if not part of the whole, hatched from the fear of remaining alone? An "other" is nothing more than a negative projection of self, something outside of the inside. In order to understand the self, we must look within—collapse the internal into the external—in order to see beyond. In other words, dissolve the self into something bigger, something infinite and without thought. This is what we mean when we refer to the *spectacle of the void*. After all, to exist is to be both imprisoned in a limited comprehension of the universe and "privileged" with the burden of consciousness. To exist is to collapse the internal into the external, to come face to face with horror.

It is this very fact that fuels our desire to create speculative images and texts of horror, to draw spectators into the web of our own misery, to spread the miasma of our dread to others. We do this, as we know, as a direct result of the horror reality, or the unconscious understanding that our limited comprehension of the universe and an inability to communicate the strangeness of the world-without-us fuels our own speculation. This speculation is often correlated with sense and memory, and the laws of the so-called natural order of things, through the act of looking. What we see—and how we see it—can only be understood as the truth, or that which is possible. Attempting to relate this so-called truth to our own existence, often understood through the language and rigor of science, leads to the opening of the void within, which connects the world-for-us and the world-without-us. Finally, in an attempt to relate this connection to others, we will only encounter the inevitable failure of language—the eradication of self; to become something other than human. This is the inevitable worst to come—*the dissolve* of correlation into the speculative unknown.

Realty is not what it used to be—this has never not been true.

# Notes

[1] Carlo Michelstaedter, *Persuasion and Rhetoric*, trans. Russell Scott Valentino, Cinzia Sartini Blum, and David J. Depew (New Haven & London: Yale University Press, 2004), xiii.

[2] Ibid., 68–9.

[3] Ibid., xiv.

[4] Brian Evenson, *Fugue State* (Minneapolis: Coffee House Press, 2009), 23.

[5] Ibid., 28.

[6] Ibid., 30.

[7] *Persuasion and Rhetoric*, 23.

[8] Nicola Masciandaro and Gary J. Shipley, "Open Commentary to Eugene Thacker's 'Cosmic Pessimism,'" *continent.* 2.2 (2012): 77.

[9] Graham Harman, "On the Horror of Phenomenology: Lovecraft and Husserl," *Collapse* IV (2012): 345.

[10] Eugene Thacker, *In the Dust of This Planet: Horror of Philosophy Vol. 1* (Winchester, UK; Washington, USA: Zero Books; 2011), 4–6.

[11] Ibid., 5.

[12] Henri Bergson, *Matter and Memory*, trans. Nancy Margaret Paul and W. Scott Palmer (New York: Zone Books, 1988), 17.

[13] Ibid., 21.

[14] Ibid., 66.

[15] Georges Bataille, *The Story of the Eye*, trans. Joachim Neugroschel (San Francisco: City Lights Books, 2001), 82.

[16] Ibid., 91.

[17] *Matter and Memory*, 35.

[18] Quentin Meillassoux, *After Finitude: An Essay on the Necessity of Contingency*, trans. Ray Brassier (London: Bloomsbury, 2013), 27.

[19] Emmanuel Levinas, *On Escape*, trans. Bettina Bergo (Stanford: Stanford University Press, 2003), p. 53.

[20] Ibid., 53.

[21] J. G. Ballard, *War Fever* (New York: Farrar, Straus and Giroux; 1991), 128.

[22] *Persuasion and Rhetoric*, 26.

[23] *War Fever*, 128.

[24] H. P. Lovecraft, *The Call of Cthulhu and Other Weird Stories*, ed. S. T. Joshi (New York: Penguin Books, 1999), 167.

[25] Ibid., 170.

[26] H. P. Lovecraft, *The Dreams in the Witch House and Other Weird Stories*, ed. S. T. Joshi (New York: Penguin Books, 2004), 303.

[27] Ibid., 24.

[28] H. P. Lovecraft, *The Thing on the Doorstep and Other Weird Stories*, ed. S. T. Joshi (New York: Penguin Books, 2001), 271.

[29] Michel Houellebecq, *H.P. Lovecraft: Against the World, Against Life*, trans. Dorna Khazeni (San Francisco: Believer Books, 2005), 66.

[30] *After Finitude*, 82.

[31] George Sieg, "Infinite Regress Into Self-Referential Horror: The Gnosis of the Victim," *Collapse* IV (2012): 32.

[32] Arthur Machen, *The White People and Other Weird Stories*, ed. S.T. Joshi (New York: Penguin Books, 2011), 300.

[33] *After Finitude*, 82.

[34] Ibid., 85.

[35] *The Call of Cthulhu and Other Weird Stories*, 139.

[36] Graham Harman, *Weird Realism: Lovecraft and Philosophy* (Winchester UK; Washington, USA: Zero Books; 2012), 122–23.

[37] Friedrich Nietzsche, *The Birth of Tragedy*, trans. Shaun Whiteside (New York: Penguin Books, 2003), 22.

[38] Ibid., 26.

[39] Ibid., 32.

[40] Roger B. Salomon, *Mazes of the Serpent: An Anatomy of Horror Narrative* (Ithaca: London; Cornell University Press, 2002), 32.

[41] *The Birth of Tragedy*, 113.

[42] Thomas Ligotti, *The Conspiracy Against the Human Race* (New York: Hippocampus Press, 2010), 120.

[43] Ibid., 167.

[44] Ibid., 93.

[45] *Mazes of the Serpent*, 20.

[46] Ibid., 22.

[47] Ibid., 22.

[48] Joyce Carol Oates; "The King of Weird"; review of *H.P. Lovecraft: A Life*, by S. T. Joshi; *The Dunwich Horror and Others*, selected by August Derleth, ed. S. T. Joshi; *At the Mountains of Madness & Other Novels*, ed. S. T. Joshi; *Dagon and Other Macabre Tales*, ed. S. T. Joshi; *Miscellaneous Writings*, ed. S. T. Joshi; *Selected Letters Vol. I: 1911–1924*, ed. S. T. Joshi; *Selected Letters Vol. II: 1925–1929*, ed. S. T. Joshi; *Selected Letters Vol. III: 1929–1931*, ed. S. T. Joshi; *Selected Letters Vol. IV: 1932–1934*, ed. S. T. Joshi; and *Selected Letters Vol. V: 1934–1937*, ed. S. T. Joshi; *The New*

*York Review of Books*; October 31, 1986.
http://www.nybooks.com/articles/archives/1996/oct/31/the-king-of-weird/

[49] Friedrich Nietzsche, *Beyond Good and Evil*, trans. R. J. Hollingdale (New York: Penguin Books, 2003), 102.

[50] *The Conspiracy Against the Human Race*, 145.

[51] Neil Bartlett, 'Watching Salò,' included in the booklet accompanying the Criterion Collection DVD edition *Salò, or the 120 Days of Sodom*, 2011, 14.

[52] Ibid., 14.

[53] Ibid., 16.

[54] Maurice Blanchot, *The Space of Literature*, trans. Ann Smock (Lincoln, Nebraska; London: University of Nebraska Press; 1989), 32.

[55] Ibid., 30.

[56] *Mazes of the Serpent*, 76.

[57] Arthur Schopenhauer, *The World as Will and Presentation: Volume One*, trans. Richard E. Aquila, David Carus (New York: Pearson Longman, 2008), 335.

[58] *The Space of Literature*, 95.

[59] Ibid., 91.

[60] Gary J. Shipley, "Remote Viewing: Observations Inspired or Furthered by *And They Were Two In One and One In Two*" in *And They Were Two In One and One In Two* (Schism Press, 2014), 141.

[61] *Matter and Memory*, 139.

[62] Julia Kristeva, *Powers of Horror: An Essay on Abjection* (New York: Columbia University Press, 1982), 209.

[63] Reza Negarestani, *Cyclonopedia: Complicity with Anonymous Materials* (Melbourne: re.press, 2008), 43.

[64] Ibid., 44.

[65] Ibid., 44.

[66] "On the Horror of Phenomenology: Lovecraft and Husserl," 342.

[67] *The Call of Cthulhu and Other Weird Stories*, 139.

[68] *After Finitude*, 28.

[69] *Cyclonopedia*, 61.

[70] Junji Ito, *Gyo, Vol. 1* (San Francisco: Viz Media, 2003), 192.

[71] Ibid., 194.

[72] Ibid., 196.

[73] Ibid., 197.

[74] Ibid., 197.

[75] Ibid., 198.
[76] Ibid., 204.
[77] Brian Evenson, *Windeye* (Minneapolis: Coffee House Press, 2012), 69.
[78] Ibid., 71.
[79] Ibid., 72.
[80] Ibid., 77.
[81] Ibid., 78.
[82] *The World as Will and Presentation: Volume One*, 330.
[83] *The Space of Literature*, 133–34.
[84] Hans Henny Jahnn, *The Living Are Few, The Dead Many* (London: Atlas Press, 2012), 83.
[85] Ibid., 83.
[86] Ibid., 84.
[87] Ibid., 86.
[88] Ibid., 90.
[89] Ibid., 94.
[90] Ibid., 97–8.
[91] Ibid., 99.
[92] Ibid., 106.
[93] Ibid., 113.
[94] Ibid., 114.
[95] Ibid., 122.
[96] Ibid., 132.
[97] Ibid., 137.
[98] Ibid., 138.
[99] Ibid., 140.
[100] Ibid., 144–5.
[101] Ibid., 146.
[102] Ibid., 149.
[103] Ibid., 159.
[104] Ibid., 163.
[105] *The Space of Literature*, 31.
[106] *In the Dust of This Planet*, 9.
[107] Ray Brassier, "The Enigma of Realism: On Quentin Meillassoux's *After Finitude*," *Collapse* II (2007): 18.
[108] Ibid., 41.

[109] Ray Brassier, "Concepts and Objects," *The Speculative Turn: Continental Materialism and Realism*, eds. Levi Bryant, Nick Srnicek, and Graham Harman, (Melbourne: re.press, 2011), 63.
[110] *The Conspiracy Against the Human Race*, 102.
[111] *The World as Will and Presentation: Volume One*, 179.
[112] Laird Barron, *The Imago Sequence and Other Stores* (San Francisco: Night Shade Books, 2007), 38.
[113] Ibid., 53.
[114] Ibid., 54.
[115] Ibid., 66.
[116] Ibid., 76.
[117] *The Space of Literature*, 240.
[118] *In the Dust of This Planet*, 120.
[119] Ray Brassier, *Nihil Unbound: Enlightenment and Extinction* (Basingstoke, UK: Palgrave Macmillan, 2007), 238.
[120] *In the Dust of This Planet*, 125.
[121] Ibid., 132.
[122] Laird Barron, *Occultation and Other Stories* (San Francisco: Night Shade Books, 2010), 25.

Also available from SCHISM press:

## *True Detection*

Edited by Edia Connole, Paul J. Ennis, and Nicola Masciandaro.

"The most intelligent series in TV history has opened strange crypts for explorers. This excellent essay collection reveals just how far the dark tunnels lead. Let it coax you from the comforts of death and fear, into detection of the guttering nightmare that is life, coldly seen." Nick Land

## *Sufficient Unto the Day: Sermones Contra Solicitudinem*

By Nicola Masciandaro.

The writings in this volume are bound by desire to refuse worry, to reject and throw it away the only way possible, by means that are themselves free from worry. If this is impossible—all the more reason to do so.

## *And They Were Two In One And One In Two*

Edited by Nicola Masciandaro and Eugene Thacker.

A collection of essays on beheading and cinema, with full color interior. Contents: Dominic Pettman, "What Came First, the Chicken or the Head?" - Eugene Thacker, "Thing and No-Thing" - Alexi Kukuljevic, "Suicide by Decapitation" - Alexander Galloway, "The Painted Peacock" - Evan Calder Williams, "Recapitation" - Nicola Masciandaro, "Decapitating Cinema" - Ed Keller, "Corpus Atomicus" - Gary J Shipley, "Remote Viewing." Photography by Leighton Pierce.

SCHISM